Just Like You

Chris Dessi

Contents

INTRODUCTION iv

RUSS ADLER
Owner, Law Offices of Russell E. Adler Pllc 1

LISA BESSERMAN
Founder, Startup Buenos Aires... 14

TAMI CANIZZARO
Head of Marketing, eBay Enterprise 24

JOHN DOKES
Chief Marketing Officer at AccuWeather 33

TIM FLANNERY
VC & Operator 42

CHRIS GUERRERO
CrossFit Affiliate Head-Trainer & Owner 51

SHEILA HAILE
Chief Marketing Officer at Cohen's Fashion Optical 62

JOHN HALL,
CEO, Influence & CO. #72 FORBES'
"America's Most Promising Companies" 71

CHRIS HANSEN
TV Journalist & Author 81

JEFFREY HAYZLETT
Primetime TV & Radio Host, Keynote Speaker,
Best-Selling Author, and Global Business Celebrity 92

DAVE KERPEN
Founder & CEO, Likeable Local,
NY Times Best-Selling Author & Speaker 101

OREN KLAFF
Author of Pitch Anything,
Managing Director at Intersection Capital 111

BILL LAROSA
CEO/Executive Leadership Coach,
Business/Personal Growth Consultant,
Experienced Public Board Director & Angel Investor 119

LEW LEONE
VP and General Manager at WNYW/WWOR-TV 131

CHRIS MALONEY
U.S. Marine, Pilot, Co-founder at Cause Engine 143

TODD MARKS
CEO, President, and Founder Mindgrub 153

JEFF PEARLMAN
Best Selling Author 163

ROSHINI RAJ, MD
Medical Host, Author, Co-Founder of TULA 179

RAYMOND A. SANSEVERINO
Chair of Loeb & Loeb's Real Estate Department 188

ROSANNA SCOTTO
Anchor of Good Day New York 203

DENNIS SIMMONS
CEO at Wasc Holding LLC 211

TOM SHINE
Serial Entrepreneur, Co-Founder Logo Athletic,
Executive Leadership Reebok, XIX Entertainment,

Angel Investor 224

JIM TREACY
Public Speaker, Writer, Consultant and
Former President and COO of Monster Worldwide 234

ADRIAN DESSI 250

Introduction

My Father's last words to me were "keep up the good work." I hold those words close to my heart. They're my mantra for my business and personal life alike. Dad lived for five years with Lou Gehrig's disease (ALS). The disease took his life in Feb of 2015.

In May of 2013, NY Times Best Selling Author Jeff Pearlman conducted an interview with my Father on the pages of his blog in a section called the "Quaz." In Jeff's "Quaz" he peppers people who interest him with compelling and unusual questions. It was a powerful view into what my Father was dealing with while battling ALS. Jeff's "Quaz" is what inspired me to conduct the interviews you're about to read. Jeff has agreed to let me share that interview with my Father Adrian as the final (24th) interview.

For 40 years, my brother Mark and I had our Father's advice all to ourselves. We were eager students. We absorbed his tutelage. Following his lead at every turn. We approached our careers with fervor. We attacked our education with hyper focus. We climbed the corporate ladder and excelled. Dad was at the epicenter of our world. Dad was my biggest fan in business. He was my confidant and mentor. In the past, I would turn to my Father for every manner of advice. When you read his interview, you'll understand why. Now that he's gone, I find myself seeking, seeking the wisdom of those who have lived more, seen more, and experienced more. Today I turn to my network of inspiring colleagues and friends.

I found people that I felt have been successful from all walks of life. I asked them about success, their personal journey, and how they define success. I did so because I believe that success is rarely linear. I also think that many people have a varied definition of success. To some success means monetary gain. To others, it means meditation for two hours a day. Even others seek to spend as much time outdoors doing what they love.

In the subsequent pages, you will take a journey. One filled with hardship, setbacks, and some triumphs. There are no Hollywood endings here. No swelling music with protagonists riding off into the sunset. Just real life gut wrenching experiences from real people.

As you flip through the interviews, you'll begin to see patterns emerging. There is a rhythm to success. A dance filled with focus, discipline, work ethic, resiliency, optimism, self-believe, and motivation. This publication is not a playbook by any stretch. What's worked for one became a colossal failure for another. I encourage you to read with an open mind and heart. Approach each interview as a new way to view your world. Pull what you can; leave behind what won't work for you. Continue to come back to these pages for inspiration. See yourself in every story, and define your path to success.

In Adrian Dessi's memory, 10% of all proceeds from this book will go towards ALS combating research.

I want you to keep up your work. I hope this book makes a meaningful impact in that journey for you.

To learn more about Chris Dessi please visit:

http://www.christopherdessi.com
and
http://www.silverbacksocial.com

Exceptional Success from a Unique Talent

RUSS ADLER

Owner, Law Offices of Russell E. Adler Pllc

I'm not an attorney, but attorneys surround me in my family life. I have three family members who practice law. When attorneys surround you, you tend to see patterns. Patterns of behavior. Patterns of thought. Patterns in their approach to life. I can spot an attorney from miles away. They're paid to look at the negative. Point out the downside. Advise against risk. This perspective is a great thing, but not *my thing*. I get it; I respect it, but it's just not the way my brain works.

My friend Russ is an attorney. Russ doesn't look like an attorney. Russ doesn't behave like an attorney. Russ exhibits none of the patterns of "attorney like" behavior that I've seen in my life. I believe that's why he draws me to him. Russ and I met while he was in law school with my brother. He's now *my attorney*. Whatever that means. He's also a dear friend, and he's running his practice on his terms. I admire that. I also admire that he's different than most.

- Attorneys wear black wing tips. I've seen Russ wear red shoes.
- Attorneys are members of golf clubs. Russ competes in CrossFit "battles." Attorneys go to the ballet. Russ jams on his red electric guitar.
- Attorneys drive big black Mercedes. Russ drives an orange Mini Cooper.
- Attorneys take meetings in huge offices with oak furniture. My last meeting with Russ took place outside on his deck while we both admired the woods in his backyard, sipping coffee. His lovely wife and two daughters made a guest appearance.

Russ has his own unique patterns of behavior. Russ is more of an entrepreneur than an attorney. When Russ gives me advice (legal or otherwise), I take it.

There are many attorneys out there. Russ isn't like any of them. That's why he's my attorney. He's the high hat of the beat. The risk taker in a sea of conservatives. I think these differences are why I'm drawn to Russ. They're the reason he has become more of a *"consigliere"* to me than hired gun. He's the real deal. Genuine, grounded and a new kind of attorney with a new kind of approach to success that I thought worth sharing. I think you'll agree.

Chris Dessi: You worked at four large law firms over the course of a decade before starting your own labor and employment law firm. Tell us about what the catalyst for that decision and the pros/cons of your choice.

Russ Adler: The firms I had worked at over the 13 years before I started my own practice were very diverse in terms of, size or culture, for example, but they were also uniform to a significant degree. By that I mean the emphasis on quantity over quality that is inherent in a business model built purely on the billable hour. For years, the appeal of law firms was that if you worked hard and put in 7-10 years, you'd make partner, and you were "set." That is far from the case, nor has it been for many years. As one friend of mine put it: a law firm partnership is like a pie eating contest, where the reward is more pie. I always felt that I had the right skill set to go out on my own, but the biggest obstacle was fear of failure. When I made the leap, it was one week before my 40th birthday, I have two kids, a mortgage, and my wife had not been working for about five years at the time. I would have been crazy not to be afraid. Once I made the decision, I knew that I had to be 100% committed and fearless.

When I compare my professional life now to what it was when I was an employee, I can honestly say there are only pros, no cons. I have control over my practice and, therefore, control over my personal life. I have the freedom to say "no" to clients I don't want to represent and to do the work I enjoy. Yes, there is stress in having my own practice, but I'd take that type of stress over the stress that comes with employment where you are in many ways at the mercy of others.

Chris Dessi: We have a friend who graduated from your alma mater of St. Johns Law in 2011. He eventually was hired by a firm that you used to work for, but it wasn't easy. More and more, we hear about attorneys having a hard time finding employment out of school. If you were graduating college today, knowing what you know now, would you still pursue a law degree? What advice do you have for those entering the legal world now?

Russ Adler: I wouldn't dissuade the 1996 Russell Adler from law school because I'm in an excellent place now and that is unquestionably a direct result of my degree. Had you asked me that question 5 years ago, perhaps the answer would be different. I know a lot of unhappy lawyers, but the majority of happy lawyers I know are solo or small firm practitioners. I think the bloom is off the rose on so-called "biglaw" practice concerning job satisfaction and work-life balance.

My advice for a newly minted lawyer is simple: listen, learn, ask lots of questions and value your reputation above all else; your reputation is the most important currency you have as a professional1. Young lawyers need to understand that even in the beginning of their careers, they are planting seeds for their future success. All the people they interact with, friends, clients, adversaries, are prospective clients or referral sources. The best compliment I get is when someone I was previously adverse to in a case later hires or recommends me.

Russ competing in the Valentine's Day Massacre — Feb 2015

Chris Dessi: You recently completed your L1 Certification as a Cross Fit Trainer. Those who read my blog regularly know that I'm addicted to CrossFit — which is indirectly because of you. (Author's note: Russ invited my brother Mark to drop into one of Russ's classes, and my brother sold me on the benefits of CrossFit). Talk to us about the role fitness plays in your career and why CrossFit works for you?

Russ Adler: I started working out when I was 17, but men our age all did the same thing back then: back and biceps on Monday, chest, and triceps on Wednesday, etc. Frankly, it was boring. I discovered CrossFit two years ago and for me it just clicked. The constant variety, mental and physical challenge and sense of community you get from CrossFit is something I never experienced, particularly since I did not play team sports in school.

I am a morning person, so I'm generally at the 5:30 am class. I love the feeling of having a great workout and being home before my kids even wake up. The people that gravitate to CrossFit tend to be dedicated, and perhaps a little crazy, but I think that level of dedication is necessary for fitness and your career. I took the Cross-Fit Level One certification course because I wanted to improve my CrossFit knowledge and coach classes at my box (CrossFit-speak for "gym") on occasion. I enjoy the coaching/mentor dynamic, and I get the same satisfaction giving career advice to a young lawyer or colleague as I do when I coach CrossFit.

Chris Dessi: How important are habits and routine to your success? What is your Rhythm? What time do you go to bed? Do you meditate?

Russ Adler: Running my own firm, or any business for that matter, requires discipline. When you're the one setting the agenda, it's easy to get distracted, so I do rely on routines and habits to keep me focused. About my day, I get up at 4:50 am during the week if I'm working out, maybe 5:45 if I'm not. I like to be in bed by 10:30-11:00 at the latest. When I'm working, I don't allow myself to get distracted by personal matters. I rarely make personal calls during traditional work hours and my wife will tell you that I'm not very good at handling those types of things while I'm in "work mode." Throughout the day, I am constantly updating my "to do" list and calendar. I spend a lot of time staying organized, perhaps too much time, but I feel better knowing that I've mapped out what I have to do and when I have to do it, and that information is always at my fingertips. I am not a procrastinator; I have too much going on in a typical day to put something aside, I'd rather get it done so I can tackle the next project. I don't meditate; my version of meditation is CrossFit.

Chris Dessi: We are both blessed with two beautiful little girls. As a parent, what can you do on a day to day basis for your girls to help prepare them for future success?

Russ Adler: Thank you. The majority of the credit for my girls goes to my wife Andrea, she's just phenomenal with them. Now that my girls are getting older (8 and 6), I often tell them that it's not my job to do everything for them, it's my job to teach them how to do everything for themselves. The main thing I try to instill into my kids is self-confidence. To me, it's the most important thing you can pass on as a parent. Confident kids make better decisions in all aspects of their lives.

Chris Dessi: For people like yourself who have seen great monetary success — what do you think is dangerous about that type of success?

Russ Adler: Great is a relative term, but it's been a good year and I hope that I can sustain it for another 20 years, give or take. There is a certain level of income you need depending on your community. In Westchester County, where we live, the bar is set high. But once you surpass that "number," it's just a question of degree. I don't think the person who makes $1 million is twice as happy as the person who makes $500,000.

I remember reading in *Bonfire of the Vanities*, that the main character made $1 million — and this was the 80's so let's assume that's $5 million now — and he explains all these expenses and obligations that came with it and how it was, in effect, a gilded cage. Money gives some people a false sense of intelligence and importance. I know people who are infatuated with others because of what they have, not who they are. I have friends who are all over the economic spectrum, and I don't let that factor into my opinion of them as people.

Chris Dessi: I speak with many successful executives that question the value of college. You were law school class-mates with my brother Mark, what do you say to those detractors of education?

Russ Adler: I question the excessive emphasis we have in our culture with lists and ranking of colleges and univer-sities, the kind that, for example, U. S. News and World Report issues every year. I also put a lot of stock in life experience. My greatest learning experiences came from waiting tables for seven years during college and law school and backpacking through the Middle East for four months when I was 22. I think our educational system should place greater emphasis on developing real-world skills. For exam-ple, every high school and college should teach classes on things like understanding mortgages, credit cards, leasing an apartment or car, saving for retirement, etc.

Theory has its place, but there is an absence of focus on real-world application throughout the system.

Chris Dessi: How do you define success?

Russ Adler: For me, it's self-determination — the ability to dictate my own path professionally. I'm about to mark my third anniversary and the freedom I have now, compared to my former professional life, is what sticks out as the most notable difference, and what I value most.

Russ's family

Chris Dessi: Can you explain the impact social networking/digital media has made on your business/career and you personally?

Russ Adler: It's certainly a larger presence than I would have guessed a few years ago. It is a fantastic tool for connecting with people — just last week I referred a potential case to someone I worked with 12 years ago because I found her on LinkedIn. I am fairly active on social media, mainly Facebook, and it has helped me grow my business both directly and indirectly. By directly, I mean I've been referred clients through social media contacts, and indirectly through the branding that you can establish through social media posts. Two months ago, I achieved an excellent result for a client and posted a picture of a picture of a bottle of champagne I was opening to celebrate, and that post had the most "likes" of anything I'd posted in years.

Chris Dessi: How much of your success was due to luck? Or are you of the mindset that you create your luck?

Russ Adler: I'm definitely in the latter camp. However, I think the notion of karma is spot on. If you conduct yourself the right way, be nice to people, helpful, respectful, etc. , and then others will respond in a similar fashion. That's not the same as luck. I've never believed there is a great cosmic plan or that things happen for a reason; you just have to make the most of the situations you're in.

Chris Dessi: When did you first think of yourself as a success?

Russ Adler: It was a few months after I started the practice and I realized that I was doing it — establishing a sustainable practice on my terms and already on track financially to exceed what I'd made the prior year as an employee. It wasn't one specific moment, case or outcome, but an overall realization that I was charting my own course. My father says that the 40's are your best decade because you are (hopefully) in a good place vis-à-vis your career, relationship, family, and health. I completely agree.

Chris Dessi: Many young executives who read my blog struggle with work life/balance — myself included. What advice do you give them? How do you strike a balance?

Russ Adler: As a solo practitioner, you are always "on" to some degree. That is, you are either thinking about a work issue in the back of your mind or representing your brand (yourself) in your daily interactions. For me, the key is having a supportive partner, and I have that with Andrea, and having some personal outlet, a hobby or passion, where you can turn off your "work brain."

I think companies now pretend to care about work-life balance, but it's often just a marketing tool. For younger people, I recommend they focus on managing their superiors' expectations, then deliver great results so their superiors can be at ease and know that the result will be excellent. After a time, they will be given greater leeway and start to achieve a better balance. Last, sometimes you just need to ignore the flood of emails, texts and calls and disconnect; most things can wait a little longer.

Chris Dessi: On paper, your resume reads like success. Can you tell us about your biggest failure(s)? How did it change you or shift your approach moving forward?

Russ Adler: I changed jobs once solely for money. It made me realize that the cost of greater financial success is outweighed by the stress and unhappiness it can bring. That experience instilled in me the philosophy that personal satisfaction and happiness are more valuable than economic success.

Chris Dessi: Who has been the greatest positive influence on your life? Tell us about that person.

Russ Adler: My kids. Children force us to be less selfish, and we live in a very selfish society.

Chris Dessi: What do you think is the one characteristic that all the successful people you know share?

Russ Adler: Passion. To be truly successful at something, you have to love it. Again, I see wealthy people who are miserable, so that's not success in my view.

Chris Dessi: How has your childhood (the way you were raised, your birth order) affected your career success? Did it at all?

Russ Adler: I am the youngest of four, all of us within six years, but I never put much thought into how that affected my professional life. My siblings and I all had very different personalities and chose very different careers. I think growing up in a strong, loving, grounded family certainly helped. My father is a dentist, and he still practices, and we benefitted from the fact that since he has his own practice, he was around for us. Eating dinner together was the norm, not the exception. Perhaps that had an influence on my decision to strike out on my own. Wait, am I in therapy right now?

Chris Dessi: I know you to be a very humble person. Here is your chance to brag a bit — what has been your greatest career success to date?

Russ Adler: Because of the nature of my work, I really can't discuss any particular case or outcome. I think my greatest success to date is the fact that I've been able to build a practice from nothing to something I'm very proud of and hope to continue to build for years to come.

RAPID FIRE

Chris Dessi: My daughters know that I hate witches — what's one thing that scares the hell out of you?

Russ Adler: The Exorcist. That movie scares the crap out of me.

Chris Dessi: Best day of your life?

Russ Adler: My first kid's birth. That changed everything in my life forever.

Chris Dessi: Worst day of your life?

Russ Adler: I consider myself very fortunate to be able to say I can't think of anything that terrible in my nearly 43 years.

Chris Dessi: How many kipping pull-ups can you do (unbroken)?

Russ Adler: 39 last time I tried about a year ago. I think I can beat that now.

Chris Dessi: You're a guitar player, and seem to love your guitar. You also have a cool Mini Cooper. You have to give up one of the two things forever, which do you choose, and why?

Russ Adler: Easy, the car. You can always get more things; skills or talents are better than possessions. By the way, your question assumes I'm a good guitar player…

Chris Dessi: Name someone who knows more about you than anyone else in the world.

Russ Adler: My wife, but I don't tell her everything.

Chris Dessi: Most powerful book you've ever read that you recommend to everyone?

Russ Adler: I've never read a "self-help" or business book. I'm a fan of books where the author builds a fleshed out, vibrant and believable world, such as *Lord of the Rings* or *Dune*. For non-fiction, I always recommend *Devil in the White City* — you don't even realize it's non-fiction because it reads like a novel.

Connect with Russ on LinkedIn here
https://www.linkedin.com/in/russell-e-adler-457b865

Learn more about Russ's law practices here
http://radlerlawpllc.com/

LISA BESSERMAN

Founder, Startup Buenos Aires

Lisa Besserman and I first met during a _"Start Up Week-end."_ The event took place where I had co-working space (the Digital Arts Experience) in White Plains, New York. I spoke at that event. This chance meetup was just weeks before I launched the first-ever Westchester Digital Summit. I was immediately impressed by Lisa. She had just launched Startup Buenos Aires. Only a few weeks after meeting her, I wrote to see if she would join the Silverback team during Catalyst Week.

My CMO John and I connected with Amanda Slavin of Catalyst Creativ. Amanda invited us to co-host Catalyst

Week in Las Vegas. It was an awesomefour-day event in association with the Downtown Project.

Basically, it was a business retreat in Vegas. Tony Hsieh's Downtown Project partnered with Catalyst Creativ. Silverback (my agency) curated speakers and attendees. We got a ton of smart people in the room, we brainstormed, we networked, and we had some fun (we were in Vegas after all). Lisa took me up on my offer to attend, and we've become great friends. She's an inspiring and powerful female entrepreneur. I enjoyed this one.

Chris Dessi: How important are habits and routine to your success? What is your Rhythm? What time do you go to bed? Do you meditate?

Lisa Besserman: Everyone has different methods that to lead to their success, especially entrepreneurs. For me, the most important daily quality is being flexible. There have been times where I've had to fly to a different continent on a moment's notice, extend a trip for weeks at a time, or drop everything to solve a time sensitive issue. It is it's ability to address these unexpected turns that has allowed me to become the entrepreneur I am today. I guess you can say my "rhythm" is embracing the unexpected and being flexible in times of uncertainty. I work better at night, so I go to bed at around 1 am and start the day around 9 am, answering emails in bed. Working from home has its advantages.

Chris Dessi: I speak with many successful executives that question the value of college. What do you say to those detractors of education?

Lisa Besserman: I believe a college education is important as long as it infuses your knowledge and expands your horizons. However, If it gets in the way of creating the "next big thing" and inhibits you more than it advances you, then I believe it's ok to forgo the traditional institution of college. Many of the greatest innovators and influencers of our time have dropped out of college to pursue their dreams and have created amazing companies in the process. Personally, I embrace a college education, as mine was incredibly rewarding and enlightening, but I don't feel it's absolutely necessary.

Chris Dessi: How do you define success?

Lisa Besserman: To me, success isn't defined by the amount of money in your bank account, or how high one climbs the proverbial corporate ladder. I believe success is defined by the lives we touch. Success can be measured by the impact we make towards building a better world, and doing our part to inspire those around us to achieve *greatness*.  The possibility of doing so is endless, and the value is unquantifiable. Success is doing what you love, doing it well, and doing good in the world.

Chris Dessi: You've traveled to 50 Countries, in many of which you did mission work. When did you start to notice that you had a passion for travel? Also, talk to us about how throughout your career you managed to connect travel and business.

Lisa Besserman: My first trip abroad was to Israel at the age of 15. It was my first (and last) organized trip. From there, I had a serious case of wanderlust and knew I needed to see as much of the world as humanly possible. There are so many beautiful cultures, languages, cities, and people all around the globe, I knew I wanted to explore and learn as much as possible, and no better way to do that than travel. I've always had a knack for leadership and loved business, so when I went to university, I decided to major in International Business, knowing it would allow me to travel globally while doing business. After I had graduated college, I worked in Japan for two years, came back to NYC, worked at a startup, then moved to  Argentina and wound up creating my organization abroad, as an expat entrepreneur.

Chris Dessi: You've been in Argentina for almost three years now. How does the business scene differ from America? What are some things you like more and some things that you wished were the same as in the US.

Lisa Besserman: Torsten Kolind, CEO of YouNoodle, and personal friend presented at the Latam Startup Conference, and his first slide read: "Latin America, where creativity meets inefficiency." To me, that sums up the region quite poetically. Argentina is home to some of the greatest entrepreneurial and tech talent I've ever seen in my life, there's a contagious energy in the city, and it truly inspires me to create and innovate on a regular basis. I've never felt this inspiration anywhere else in the world.

Additionally, there's a large emphasis on relationships, especially when doing business. A focus on relationships has its benefits and drawbacks. On the positive side, you get to know a person multi-dimensionally, which has the potential of making business and collaborations run smoother and stronger. On the other hand, the emphasis on relationships is sometimes at the cost of efficiency, speed, and execution, which can be a major hindrance in business. There's also a very distinct different definition of time in Latin America. This definition of time is something that varies quite substantially between cultures and regions. Showing up late to meetings, or starting events late is a regular occurrence in Latin America, as is not responding to emails for weeks at a time. For a fast-paced New Yorker, this can be a challenge to navigate, and has been learning experience when assimilating to the local culture. I think one of the reasons SUBA has grown so rapidly and has become such a powerful organization, is because we were able to fuse the business cultures of the US and Argentina together, to get the best out of both.

Chris Dessi: You accomplished so much before you turned 30 — what does success in the next decade look like for you?

Lisa Besserman: I'd love to take the lessons I've learned and utilize them to help grow startup ecosystems around the world. Building a more connected global startup community and continuing to provide tools, resources and mentorships to fellow entrepreneurs is a dream of mine that I'm always working towards. As I mentioned earlier, success is defined by the lives we touch and the impact we make in this world, I'd love to continue the path I'm on, on a much larger and scalable platform.

Chris Dessi: You've done so much in the way of helping startups — what is it that attracts you to businesses that are just starting to take off?

Lisa Besserman: The endless possibilities. It's the incredible way that companies start off as mere ideas, but have the potential to transform into amazing things.

Chris Dessi: Can you explain the impact, that social networking/digital media has made on your business/career or you personally?

Lisa Besserman: Digital media creates a borderless audience and allows missions to become movements, and words to become actions. Working with, and connecting global startup ecosystems is possible given the reach and impact that we receive from digital media, social networks, and online communities.

Chris Dessi: How much of your success was due to luck? Or are you of the mindset that you create your luck?

Lisa Besserman: I absolutely believe in dumb luck, but I'm more of a fan of smart luck. I think a recipe for success is crafted through calculated risks, trusting in your vision, being flexible in your execution, knowing your market, sprinkled with a little bit of luck. Most successful entrepreneurs will not attribute their success to mostly luck, it's mostly hard work, sweat, and dedication. However, a little bit of luck always plays a role in the execution, and can go a long way.

Chris Dessi: When did you first think of yourselves as a success, or do you feel like you need to accomplish more first?

Lisa Besserman: I think the moment we start thinking of ourselves as successful, is the moment we stop striving for success. It's also such a multi-faceted word, which makes it hard to measure. I believe I've accomplished a lot in my years and have had many triumphs, but I also believe I have a long way to go. I suppose once I'm on the cover of Forbes I'll be able to give in and finally call myself "successful."

Chris Dessi: Many young executives who read my blog struggle with work life/balance. How do you strike a balance?

Lisa Besserman: This is one of my favorite topics. Whenever I give talks or presentations, I always try to incorporate something on the topic of balance. When I started out as an entrepreneur, nobody warned me about the extreme highs and lows faced on a daily basis. Being an entrepreneur has caused me to experience more emotions than anything else in my life. It's important to have a strong support system and a network of people you love and trust that will help you stabilize and balance yourself. It's hard not to get sucked into the vortex of creating, coding, building, working, etc. but it's necessary. If you don't find that balance, you'll burn out, or worse. Having a strong support system is the best way to find that balance, and force you to step away from the computer from time to time. I schedule weekly gym sessions, monthly date nights with my husband and friends and do my best to sign mentally offline when I should be present in life outside of work. It may be difficult to step away, but it's important, it helps you gain necessary perspective and allows you to re-energize yourself, which will create major benefits in the long run. It's crucial to find things that you love doing outside of work, and mix those into your daily life, whether it be a new hobby, learning a new skill, or just unplugging.

Chris Dessi: Who has been the greatest positive influence on your life? Tell us about that person.

Lisa Besserman: As cliche as it may sound, my mother. Before I was born, my father was involved in a car accident that left him disabled. My mother held our family together emotionally and financially. She is the hardest worker I've ever seen, who fully dedicates herself to everything and everyone she loves. She's raised three kids, taken care of our disabled father, and her mother who suffered from Alzheimer's while working full-time and supporting our entire family. Incredibly, she did it all with a smile and inspired us to not only accept challenges but overcome obstacles to achieve our dreams. She's the most positive and kind-hearted person I've ever met, and for these reasons she's the most positive influence in my life.

Chris Dessi: What do you think is the one characteristic that all the successful people you know share?

Lisa Besserman: Perseverance

Chris Dessi: As a woman in business, have you ever experienced discrimination — how has that affected your outlook, and drive to succeed?

Lisa Besserman : I've been fortunate to be a minority in a field while never felling discrimination. I expected some push back when creating Startup Buenos Aires because it was a community movement that required the city to get behind me and my crazy mission. I anticipated that being a foreigner and a woman would work against me in a multitude of ways, but thankfully it has not. The only issue I've faced was when I created SUBA and would frequently ask to meet with influential members of the community, many of which were men. Given the business society in Argentina, it was common to meet over drinks, rather than in offices. On more than one occasion, I found myself on accidental dates, rather than business meetings. Somehow the tone of the meeting shifted, and I found myself in unexpected romantic situations, rather than the business meetings I proposed. At the time, I was single, so it wasn't a problem, now I make the agenda clear, as well as my marital status, so there's no confusion.

Chris Dessi: How has your childhood (the way you were raised, your birth order) affected your career success? Did it at all?

Lisa Besserman: I'm a classic middle child. I've always been very independent, curious, and an overachieving perfectionist. I think that profoundly affected who I am today because I felt a strong need to create a voice for myself. Additionally, I was the only one of my siblings to go away to college, live abroad, and make a frequent lifestyle out of leaving the country.

Chris Dessi: Here is your chance to brag a bit — what has been your greatest career success to date?

Lisa Besserman: Building a strong startup community and ecosystem in Buenos Aires, Argentina, as a foreigner

RAPID FIRE

Chris Dessi: My daughters know that I hate witches — what's one thing that scares the hell out of you?

Lisa Besserman: Death.

Chris Dessi: Best day of your life?

Lisa Besserman: My Wedding

Chris Dessi: Worst day of your life?

Lisa Besserman: The death of my grandfather

Chris Dessi: Who is your hero?

Lisa Besserman: My mother

Chris Dessi: What is the best gift you've ever been given?

Lisa Besserman: A plane ticket to Europe for my first solo back-packing trip

Chris Dessi: Do you collect anything?

Lisa Besserman: Stamps on my passport and magnets from countries visited.

Chris Dessi: What motivates you to work as hard as you do?

Lisa Besserman: Success (see definition above)

Chris Dessi: Name someone who knows more about you than anyone else in the world.

Lisa Besserman: My sister

Chris Dessi: Most powerful book you've ever read that you recommend to everyone?

Lisa Besserman: The Alchemist by Paulo Coelho

Lisa Besserman: https://www.linkedin.com/in/lisabesserman

Facebook: http://www.facebook.com/lisabesserman

A Corporate Success with an Entrepreneurial Flare

TAMI CANIZZARO
Head of Marketing, eBay Enterprise

Tami Canizzaro is a unique executive — dynamic and inspiring on one hand, down to earth, and practical on the other. I've been fortunate to get to know Tami over the past two years. She spoke at my event the Westchester Digital Summit and since then has become a friend. She has climbed the ranks of corporate American while maintaining a family and a strong sense of who she is. I find her inspiring. As the father of two little girls, I look to women like Tami as beacons of what can be for my daughters. When we first met, she was an executive at IBM. Today she is part of a powerhouse intellectual stronghold at Ebay. They're shaking things up, and Tami is leading the charge. If you're a woman in Corporate America, you must follow Tami on social media. Forbes recently honoted her as one of the 10 Keynote Speakers Who Will Keep You Ahead of Digital Marketing Trends. She keeps an active blog that offers practical insight into a modern marketers mind, all while adding a charming sense of reality with each post. I'm thrilled to introduce Tami as one of my success interviews. She's a powerful woman leading the charge, and her interview does not disappoint.

Chris Dessi: You have a thriving blog and an impressive social media following. As I write this, you have over 40,000 highly engaged followers on Twitter. What advice can you give to executives that are looking to grow their social media following?

Tami Canizzaro: About seven years ago, I changed jobs at work and part of my new responsibility was to run social media. This was a personal crisis for me as I wasn't active on any platforms and I was an egg on Twitter! I had been procra stinating to engage in social media and realized that I needed to get in the game. I slowly started to build an active following on Twitter,  updated my LinkedIN profile, started posting on Facebook.

It was painstaking at first. I took my daily dose of social to learn the space. But slowly I started getting to know people virtually and making connections. It became less about counting my followers and more about meeting like-minded people and sharing ideas. I found it was a great tool to follow people in the industry who I admired. And it was a great tool to help me build my professional career and personal brand. After about six months, I got really into it. I now really enjoy writing my blog, and I love running into people who know me as @TamiCann from Twitter. I find bloggers have a community bond, and it's given me status as a forward thinking marketer who gets the power of social.

Chris Dessi Did you ever receive any negative feedback from your superiors about your blogging and social media activity in general? What advice can you offer other high-ranking executives about blogging and navigating the checks and balances of their organization?

Tami Canizzaro: Yes, I think it's a real concern. It's unfortunate, but some execs still see it as a waste of time. My advice is to make sure you have a management chain which is supportive or find a manager or executive sponsor who does support you. If your boss sees social as a boondoggle, don't throw caution to the wind. Tone it down, or better yet, find a new boss. My CEO at eBay Enterprise came up to me after I joined and said he loved what I was doing in social and to keep it up. That's support. Building your personal brand can make you shine but this type of visibility can also invite jealousy or negative feedback from peers or up line executives who don't get it. If you're working for someone who doesn't get social or see the value, I would be concerned they aren't a forward thinker in marketing. After all, who wants to work for an egg?

Chris Dessi: How do you define success?

Tami Canizzaro: I define success as being a respected woman in tech marketing and by having a reputation as an effective leader who executes and drives results. That's what I want people to say about me in the hallways when they think I'm not around:) Success for me is being respected in the industry. I think I'm making good progress, but I work at it every day.

Chris Dessi: I speak with many successful executives that question the value of college. You have two degrees from premier institutions (Catholic University) & (NYU). What do you say to those detractors of education? Can you point to a time when you felt you HAD to have an MBA? How much has your MBA contributed to your success?

Tami Canizzaro: I do find many corporations actively recruit from a select group of schools which certainly helps you to get a great start at a Tier 1 company. For me, the MBA from NYU definitely got me in the door. Stern had a strong job placement program with a great corporate network in New York. That said, I do think there is certainly room today to go a different route. If you are moving up  an entrepreneurial track — Ie. "I started my first company when I was 22" — this holds a lot of weight with firms — arguably more than the MBA.

Chris Dessi: What is the one skill that you needed help with when you were younger that you.

Tami Canizzaro: I would say the ability to take risks. I've always been a bit risk averse. I am loyal to a fault. I should have moved around more and chased bigger jobs. A CEO of a start-up once told me if I moved to a start-up, I should prepare to be fired, at least once! I was horrified and declined moving into the start-up world which I regret. Take a risky job before it's too late. It gets harder later in life when you have a mortgage hanging over your head. Better to end up back home for a year after your start-up went bust than never to have tried or taken a risk.

Chris Dessi: I have two young daughters. What advice can you give them that if I share this with them in 10 years you think will translate to their success?

Tami Canizzaro: I suppose it would be to think big and don't be afraid to go after your dreams. Do you want to be a CEO, president, an opera singer? Great, let's make a plan. I think many of us had just assumed those jobs belonged to someone else or worried we might not have the talent. More often, I'm guessing those jobs go to the person who had the guts to go after their dreams vs. the one with the most natural born talent. My advice would be that any job can be yours with hard work and a plan — don't settle.

Chris Dessi: In your Linkedin profile, your peers describe you as "bright, quick, intuitive, and collaborative." Do those traits come naturally to you? If not — how do you work to improve yourself?

Tami Canizzaro: I think you develop these traits over time with purposeful intent. I am always learning and working on my style. I see it as a constant evolution. I had a mentor once tell me to write down how I want to be known on my white board and to ask myself every day whether I lived up to it. My three aspirational qualities are Collaborative Executive, Innovative Change Agent, Visionary Leader. I work at it every day.

Chris Dessi: When did you first think of yourself as a success?

Tami Canizzaro: I would say I was very pleased when I received my first executive job. I felt I was being recognized as a leader within the organization. I was one of the youngest Vice Presidents at IBM and one of the few women Vice Presidents. I am proud of the fact that I'm a rising female executive in the tech industry.

Chris Dessi: What do you say to executives who love their jobs, and don't see the need to embrace social media? To put it another way — why should they care about Tweeting and blogging? How can it help them in their career? How has it helped you in yours?

Tami Canizzaro: Some executives still find social media and blogging to be frivolous. I disagree in almost all cases. People today don't listen to brands, they listen to people. Driving an active social presence for your brand is critical to a successful business. In my mind, social is now one of the most pivotal aspects of brand development and engagement with new prospects and customers. Social isn't one element of marketing — it is embedded across every element! As an executive, you should be an active spokesperson and authority for your brand.

Chris Dessi: What do you think is the one characteristic that all of the successful people you know share?

Tami Canizzaro: I think I would have to say 'drive' The drive to win in business and to be successful as an individual.

Chris Dessi: Do you have an example (s) of an opportunity that came to you just from your social media presence? That would never have come to you otherwise?

Tami Canizzaro: One tactical example — I often need to

field speakers for events. Reaching out through social has been a very effective way of reaching out to influencers and asking them to participate or speak. I am 'connected' in the industry due to my work in social in a way I would not be without it. Having the right connections within a city or vertical can be a huge help in building traction. I find it to be the secret sauce of a successful event.

Chris Dessi: How important are habits and routine to your success? What is your Rhythm? What time do you go to bed? Do you exercise? Do you meditate?

Tami Canizzaro: I find I do better with a routine. I balance a busy job with being a Mom, which can be a challenge. I got to bed pretty early — maybe 10 — and wake up early to hit the gym. I don't meditate, but I do yoga which tends to ground me. I'd do it every day if I had the time.

Chris Dessi: How important is it to your success to network with other powerful women in business? Is this an area where you flourished? Or did you do just fine networking among your male peers?

Tami Canizzaro: I would say I've had both women and men in my career who've supported me. I've also had peer executives try to block my career. I'm starting a women's networking group for executives which I'm excited about. Frankly, I don't find women support one another enough in their career growth. I'd like to play an active part in changing that.

Chris Dessi: I have an older brother. I believe that our competition growing up made me a very driven person. How has your home life affected your career success? Were your parents strict? Do you have brothers and sisters? If so, how have they affected you and your drive to succeed?

Tami Canizzaro: My father is big into sports. He was very competitive. I may have gotten some of his 'winning Is everything' gene! I don't believe my siblings affected my success. We each had very different personalities and took very different paths. I have been driven somewhat by the inequality of women in the workforce. Damn right I can do anything a man can do Chris — Maybe better:)

Chris Dessi: I know you as a humble person, but I need you to brag a little here. What has been your greatest career success to date? Tell us about it.

Tami Canizzaro: For me, starting a blog and becoming a visible presence in the marketing community is what I"m most proud of. I've made a few Forbes lists — Top 100 marketing minds and Top Digital Keynotes —which is a nice honor. Putting myself out there didn't come naturally for me, but I think it's helped my career, and I'm glad I had the courage to do it. I've had lots of great supporters along the way. Thanks Chris for being among my supporters!

RAPID FIRE

Chris Dessi: What female executive inspires you?

Tami Canizzaro: Sheryl Sandberg

Chris Dessi: Starbucks or Dunkin?

Tami Canizzaro: Starbucks (no contest)

Chris Dessi: New Jersey or New York?

Tami Canizzaro: New York

Chris Dessi: Are you a morning person?

Tami Canizzaro: Yes

Chris Dessi: Christmas or Halloween?

Tami Canizzaro: Christmas

Chris Dessi: Favorite Actor?

Tami Canizzaro: Meryl Streep

Chris Dessi: Favorite food?

Tami Canizzaro: Pizza

Chris Dessi: Favorite Alcoholic drink?

Tami Canizzaro: Red Wine

Chris Dessi: Summer or Winter?

Tami Canizzaro: Summer

Chris Dessi: Cats or dogs?

Tami Canizzaro: Dogs

Chris Dessi: Favorite business book?

Tami Canizzaro: How to Win Friends and Influence People

Chris Dessi: Favorite novel?

Tami Canizzaro: Beloved Toni Morrison

JOHN DOKES

Chief Marketing Officer at AccuWeather

For John Dokes, CMO of AccuWeather, it's all three. Talent, smarts, and good looks come naturally to John. I hate guys like that. But I just can't find it in me to hate John. He's such a good dude. But sometimes I allow myself to get irked. Like that time, a few weeks ago, when my wife and I listened to the "John Dokes Quintet" at a Jazz club called Kitano. I was angry. I approached John after his set and berated him.

"You can't be all three!" I shouted. He flinched. "What?"

I leaned in. "Dude, you *cannot* be all three." He looked at me bewildered. I stepped closer, and enunciated as I spoke "you cannot be handsome, smart, *and* talented." We both laughed. "It's not fair." It was the first time I had seen John perform live, and well — I was jealous. My wife cooed "he's so cute" while he worked the room, belting out Jazz tunes. Despite my jealousy, John's music immersed me. His band mates all creating in perfect synch. Enthralling us with their music, their style, and their all around cool vibe. It was dazzling to witness.

We mere mortals can be one of these things, sure. Two if we're lucky. But most people aren't all three. John Dokes is a triple threat — a superhero. The looks are obvious — but this dude is crazy smart too. He's also a huge musical talent. He once mentioned to me that he played music as a hobby. Lately, he's brought his talents to the lucky folks at AccuWeather where he's their Chief Marketing Officer. John is a true gentleman, a true entertainer, and a true success. The perfect person for a little chat about the idea of success, don't you think?

Let's do this.

Chris Dessi: I've known you for a few years now. You were successful when we met, and your star continues to rise. But I'm curious — when did you first consider yourself a success?

John Dokes: When I started tackling challenges outside of my comfort zone and started to see results. The first big step for me was moving from the west coast to New York to help drive initiatives at Marvel Entertainment. It was certainly a dream of mine, and when I thought about how I would make that happen, I referred to an old John H Johnson quote "Dream small dreams. If you make them too big, you get overwhelmed, and you don't do anything. If you make small goals and accomplish them, it gives you the confidence to go on to higher goals. 2 I used persistence and a focus on attainable goals to network my way into Marvel. Once inside, I was able to position myself as a problem solver and in that role it became easier to see how achievable solutions could add up to success over time.

Chris Dessi: What impact, if any has web 2.0/social media had on your success?

John Dokes: I've had the opportunity to work in industries that directly impact and enrich people's lives entertainment and now the weather. Digital has been and continues to be a critical part of building unique, close brand relationships with audiences. It has also allowed me to see a quicker return on ideas and tests that used to take years. It's an ideal situation for marketers and innovators.

When we launched AccUcast, a recent addition to Accu-Weather's award-winning app, we were struck by how much this felt like the culmination of the 1:1 marketing people have been discussing for years. It is the only interactive weather feature to offer live, crowdsourced weather maps which invite users all over the world to participate in their forecasts by providing user-submitted, current weather conditions. Our innovations team did a great job. I've always tried to highlight the innovations of really smart and passionate people and match them with an extremely engaged audience.

Chris Dessi: You're a talented musician, and you're at the pinnacle of executive leaderboards. How do you do it? To put it another way — What's your rhythm? What time do you get to bed, wake up?

John Dokes: Well, first and foremost I have a very supportive and amazing wife. She knows how to keep me focused on what's important throughout our hectic lives. My night schedule varies depending on if I have a gig that week or not. 11 pm is preferred. My alarm is set for 7 am to make sure I get the girls to school on time, though I'm usually awake by 6:30. I've been extremely fortunate to work for organizations that recognized how my other activities could enhance my value to the company. The leader of our company Dr. Joel Myers even stopped by a recent performance.

When I first started to explore my extracurricular passion of performing and recording as a jazz vocalist, I thought it would be best to keep it under wraps. A few things happened, though. One was that this thing called Youtube rendered the notion of secret public performances obsolete. The other was using all of who I am to close deals and strengthen business relationships. As my confidence grew as an artist, I started to invite more friends and colleagues to the gigs, and when I invited potential clients my deal close rate started to rise.

Chris Dessi: How important is health to you? Do you workout regularly?

John Dokes: Define regular. One of the aspects of my life that I'm focusing on more is health. Historically I've always engaged in some form of physical activity whether it's softball, baseball, soccer, dancing or a workout. As my schedule has become more hectic and travel has increased, I've found that swimming has provided the most benefits and the most opportunity when I'm traveling. I'll also occasionally find a Lindy Hop community in various locations and sneak out for a quick bout of cardio.

Chris Dessi: Wha t's your life motto?

John Dokes: Live to my potential. Create Happiness. Leave a positive legacy.

Chris Dessi: What was the single most important decision you made that contributed to your success?

John Dokes: Believing in myself. I was fortunate to have a lot of people around me who believed in me. Even some of the tougher kids in the neighborhood saw something I didn't see early on. It wasn't until I made that leap myself that I truly started to succeed.

Chris Dessi: How do you define success?

John Dokes: *Living to my potential.* I think we all have a potential that can be extended or diminished depending on the paths we choose. Each day I try to make things better on this path.

Chris Dessi: As a CMO and successful musician I get the sense that if it all went away tomorrow you could make a great living as a musician. How important do you think it is for executives to have a plan B?

John Dokes: Thanks Chris, but you clearly haven't been keeping up with the music industry. I enjoy being able to perform with some of the top musicians in the world and I see first hand how much they struggle to make a living for themselves and their families while pursuing something that they are extremely passionate about. (Support Live Music) When I meet with my mentees I try to emphasize the importance of putting yourself in a position to have options and to make sure you seize the opportunities when they come along.

Chris Dessi: What has been more rewarding, your musical endeavors, or your corporate success?

John Dokes: I'll let you know. I hope the pinnacle of each is in the future.

Chris Dessi: You have a BA from California State University-Northridge, and you are so dynamic and multi-layered as a person I'm curious: how important has education been to your success? What do you say to those that say a college education isn't worth it?

John Dokes and Stan Lee

John Dokes: Every form of education you get is worth it, and you should never stop learning whether formal or otherwise. I learned a great deal at Northridge. Their emphasis on the practical aspects of marketing allowed me to hit the ground running in my career. Growing up in East Oakland gave me the foundation to go anyplace with confidence. My time working for Ike Perlmutter at Marvel taught me to get smarter about every relevant topic, not to make decisions based on ego and to focus intensely on the bottom line. My time with Dr. Joel Myers and his brothers at AccuWeather gives me insights every day on the power of innovation and entrepreneurship.

Chris Dessi: If you could travel in time and speak with the 22 year-old John Dokes what is the one piece of advice you'd give him?

John Dokes: You will get better. Start Now.

Chris Dessi: How do you deal with adversity and setbacks? Is there a formula, or do you feel you've been able to navigate at your own pace?

John Dokes: Identify the possible paths. Choose wisely. Work hard. Repeat as necessary.

Chris Dessi: Can you point to one habit that you feel has helped to drive your success?

John Dokes: Everything can be better. Push. Push again and know when to move on.

Chris Dessi: I've seen you excel in the boardroom, and on stage. You are so comfortable in you own skin. How do you conquer moments of doubt?

John Dokes: When I'm at my best I'm listening to the people and breathing-in the situation in order to put myself in position to make the decision or give the best advice I can.

Chris Dessi: What do you think has separated you from other high performers throughout your career?

John Dokes: Well, when I think about what you might consider a high performer I'm struck more by what I admire about them and what I've learned from them. Patience, drive and a strong desire for their team and the company to succeed.

Chris Dessi: I know you as a very humble person but now is your time to brag. Tell me about some of your biggest wins.

John Dokes: My wife. My daughters. Helping to revamp the AccuWeather Brand, Relaunching Marvels Digital division, Releasing my CD, my work with Culture Shift Labs and mentoring those in need to help them get to the next level

RAPID FIRE

Chris Dessi: Did you ever had a nickname? What is it?

John Dokes: There have been a few over the years, but none have stuck. I seem to have one of those names that make people get use to saying both my first and last name together with ease.

Chris Dessi: My daughters know that I hate witches — what's one thing that scares the hell out of you?

John Dokes: Not sure fear is the right word, but I absolutely hate standing in lines. It added a bit more anxiety to the day I asked my wife to marry me. *Authors Note:* Check out John's amazing engagement story here. (http://bit. ly/1MJlOdk)

Chris Dessi: Best day of your life.

John Dokes: Today was a good day.

Chris Dessi: Worst day of your life.

John Dokes: In my teens a friend's little brother decided to chase me around the house with a gun. The gun went off. I survived with a minor injury. My jacket sleeve did not.

Now, this moment stands out as a horrible experience, but was the day worst than 9/11, or the days I lost friends and family members to guns, aids, or cancer? I still think about all of these things and try to honor their memory and acknowledge how they made me who I am today.

Chris Dessi: What is the best gift you have been given?

John Dokes: My Wedding Ring

Chris Dessi: You have access to a time machine, but you can never come back to present day. You can go into the future, or into the past. Where do you go in time?

John Dokes: I would have loved to visit the Savoy Ballroom in the 1930's, but I don't have the patience for what my life would have been like outside of the ballroom. So I'm going to say tomorrow. I expect my family and friends will be there.

Chris Dessi: Favorite alcoholic beverage?

John Dokes: Macallan 12 — Neat

Chris Dessi: Name someone who knows more about you than anyone else in the world.

John Dokes: My Wife

Chris Dessi: Most powerful business book you've ever read that you recommend to everyone.

John Dokes: Never Eat Alone

Chris Dessi: If you were a superhero, what powers would you have?

John Dokes: I am. Listening

Early Success Stories From a Vc with a Bright Future

TIM FLANNERY
VC & Operator

I'm a Loyola Greyhound. I take great pride in my alma mater. I enjoy giving back to the Loyola community. The greatest joy for me, as of late, has been networking with successful Loyola graduates. Many live in the New York metropolitan area. Many are forging careers that will help to shape the reputation of our great University. One of those former Loyola students who is moving mountains is Tim Flannery. Tim and I connected via our alumni group. We bonded during a week long trip where my agency curated attendees to the Catalyst Creativ / Tony Hsieh's downtown project event in Las Vegas. During our time there I learned about Tim's passion for his job. Tim was already rubbing elbows with some of the most powerful people in New York when we met. Now I seek his advice when investing, or advising start-ups. He's one of those guys functioning on a higher level. I really enjoy his creative approach to networking and his laid back demeanor. The guy is an intellectual powerhouse, graduating Magna Cum Laude from Loyola University Maryland. I'm proud to call the guy a friend, and I'm enjoying watching his star rise. He arguably has the best answer to my *"how do you define success"* question of any interviewee.

Chris Dessi: In 5 years you grew within one of the most known companies in the country, JP Morgan. What gave you the idea to break off and start your own venture and more importantly where did the confidence come from to take action on that idea?

Tim Flannery: My first gig at JPMorgan was in Private Equity Funds Services. I did a lot of back-office work and eventually moved to the performance and reporting side. It was my first exposure to venture capital. I wanted to get into VC one day but didn't have any specific plans. Luckily, my girlfriend-now-wife Meg introduced herself to my neighbor one day. We were having a party, she invited him over, and we became friends. A few years later, my neighbor decided to start his own fund. We stayed in touch, and he asked me to help out with a few things. Eventually, he asked me to quit my job (okay, I begged him to ask me to quit my job), and I left JPMorgan to raise my first venture fund. And it didn't take a ton of confidence. I was 27, had a very, very supportive wife, and the worst that could happen was I had to go back into finance. There was limited downside.

Chris Dessi: You began Startup Climbing as a solution to the stale networking that occurs throughout business. Frankly, it's why we started the Westchester Digital Summit. Tell us about what you consider a good networking environment?

Tim Flannery: A good networking environment should be community. People are genuinely supportive of each other and happy to be there. Often, they're connected over something personal and professional. At Startup Climbing, it's over tech and entrepreneurship plus sport. That cross section creates strong bonds And it allows people to create friendships first. They're hard to find. It's easier to identify bad networking environments. It involves an exchange of business cards, awkward conversation, and probably cheap beer and bad pizza. Enjoy your new LinkedIn connection.

Chris Dessi: Startup Climbing has taken on a life of its own. What started as networking in Brooklyn is now expanding out West and shipping up to Boston. How has your vision changed for this initiative? Talk to us about the journey from inception through this growth

Tim Flannery: Two friends and I were climbing at Brooklyn Boulders, just bemoaning the state of affairs. Climbing and hanging out seemed like more fun than another panel. A few weeks later, I threw the first Startup Climbing event, and eight other people showed. But then next month, thirty people showed. Then sixty. I never expected it to be anything but a way for me to rock climb and meet new people. Once I saw it catch on, I re-assessed. I brought on my friend Scott as my co-founder, began inviting speakers, and expanding to other locations. Now, my goal isn't to have a New York community. It's to have a community where I can travel anywhere and plug into that network at will. Now, we've got 7,000 members in 100+ cities and a ton to learn.

Chris Dessi: You have accomplished a lot in your 20s in a down economy. What is your advice to today's students on how they can create success post-college and throughout their career?

Tim Flannery: I'll share two pieces of advice my mentors gave me:

- Walk around and ask for more work. My first job at JPMorgan was transferring money between different bank accounts. I only got out of that track by bugging people and asking for stuff to do. I got good exposure and learned a lot.
- Start a blog. It's how I built up my startup/VC network. I interviewed people. I just cold emailed people I wanted to meet, asked if I could interview them, and most people said yes. Then I asked them for two more people I should meet. Now, I just write about whatever I want.

Chris Dessi: For people who have seen great monetary success — what do you think is dangerous about that type of success?

Tim Flannery: A good steady paycheck is like a drug. You get used to a certain amount of cash getting deposited into your bank account twice a month. So even if your job makes you miserable, it's tough to leave that money behind. That being said, now that I'm doing something that I love, I would have absolutely no issues about achieving great monetary success.

Chris Dessi: I speak with many successful executives that question the value of college. We both have a degree from a highly regarded Jesuit University — Loyola University Maryland. What do you say to those detractors of education?

Tim Flannery: Education is important, and anyone who says otherwise is wrong. However, it takes many forms. Higher education is one of them, and sometimes it leaves me feeling conflicted. Detractors have their points. It's four years of your life and a lot of money. If you can get the right value for that, then the other benefits that accrue are worth it. Knowledge, network personal skills, and brand are important. College is important. Not all colleges are worth it. I think we're in for a shakeup.

Chris Dessi: How do you each define success?

Tim Flannery: It's like pornography. I know it when I see it.

Chris Dessi: Can you explain the impact, that social networking/digital media has made on your business/career or you personally?

Tim Flannery: My blog changed my career trajectory. It opened more doors than I imagined. Social media has just changed how I experience events. When Hurricane Sandy hit, Twitter was my only news source. My devices and all its apps and software have become a passive extension of me.

Chris Dessi: How much of your success was due to luck? Or are you of the mindset that you create your luck?

Tim Flannery: I studied abroad in Australia instead of Ireland because I knew I'd visit Ireland some other time. I met my wife in Australia. That's pretty lucky. But, successfully wooing her was a different story. I actively try to create opportunities for chance, but chance and luck are worthless without execution. I know it doesn't answer your question, but that's the best I've got.

Chris Dessi: When did you first think of yourselves as a success?

Tim Flannery: I don't think of myself as successful. I've still got some time to go.

Chris Dessi: Many young executives who read my blog struggle with work life/balance — myself included. What advice do you give them? How do you each strike a balance?

Tim Flannery: I'm a better sprinter than marathon runner. Sometimes I need to buckle down, and most things fall to the wayside. But when things ease up, I'll grab a book and read for 48 hours straight. I'll call friends and head to a bar or relax during a weekend trip away. I don't necessarily have balance in my day-to-day, but I think I do from a broader perspective. Plus, I'm an owner in what I do, and I enjoy it. There are hard days, but it's not bad.

Chris Dessi: On paper your resumes reads like success. Can you tell us about your biggest failure(s)? How did it change you or shift your approach moving forward?

Tim Flannery: I owned a big project at JPMorgan and presented it to one of our executives. It was in good shape. I made some great progress. The executive dressed me down in front of my manager and questioned whether I belonged. Thinking I was getting fired, I went downstairs, bought some Starbursts and a lottery ticket, then just went back to my desk to fix the problem. Ultimately, the project went off smoothy, but I learned excuses don't matter. It was my Yoda moment.

Chris Dessi: Who has been the greatest positive influence on your life? Tell us about that person.

Tim Flannery: My mom. She's been through a lot and never lost her optimistic atti- tude. She's the quiet leader of my family.

Chris Dessi: What do you think is the one character- istic that all the successful people you know share?

Tim Flannery: They all like to read.

Chris Dessi: How import- ant are habits and routine to your success? What is your Rhythm? What time do you go to bed? Do you exercise? Do you meditate?

Tim Flannery: I'm a bad person to ask. I have no routines.

Chris Dessi: How has your childhood (the way you were raised, your birth order) affected your career success? Did it at all?

Tim Flannery: My parents never discouraged me from trying new things, unless there was a serious chance of physical harm. That's a helpful perspective to have later in life too.

Chris Dessi: I know you to be very humble people. Here is

your chance to brag a bit — what has been your greatest career success to date?

Tim Flannery: Closing our first fund was fun. Writing a check to my first portfolio company felt pretty good too.

RAPID FIRE

Chris Dessi: My daughters know that I hate witches — what's one thing that scares the hell out of you?

Tim Flannery: Heights

Chris Dessi: Best day of your life?

Tim Flannery: My wedding day just edges out the Phillies' 2008 World Series parade.

Chris Dessi: Worst day of your life?

Tim Flannery: My Dad passing away was a low point.

Chris Dessi: Currently when we google your name former Major League Baseball Player Tim Flannery pops up. If you were to play him in Rock, Paper, Scissor to shoot for first page on google rights what would you throw out first?

Tim Flannery: I would play the bureaucrat, all paper. By the way, he's also a baseball coach and country musician. No kidding. I was named after him. Another Tim Flannery is Australia's 2007 Man

of the Year. My SEO is terrible.

Chris Dessi: Name someone who knows more about you than anyone else in the world.

Tim Flannery: My wife.

Chris Dessi: Most powerful book you've ever read that you recommend to everyone.

Tim Flannery: IMPOSSIBLE. The Dark Tower series by Stephen King? I hate this question.

Crossfit Success: Forging Elite Fitness and Business

CHRIS GUERRERO CrossFit Affiliate
Head-Trainer & Owner

Hello, my name is Chris Dessi, and I'm a CrossFit addict. Phew. There, I said it. I didn't start off addicted to CrossFit. Like a bad after school special warning kids about the dangers of drugs, I had heard about it from some "friends". They knew I enjoyed staying fit, so they made a suggestion. "Just try it once." And just like the knucklehead kid in the after school special, I decided to give it a try. Now I'm hooked. Full blown addict. If working out is a gateway drug, CrossFit is heroin. And just like anyone else who is sick with addiction, it's hit my body hard. As I write this, my entire body is aching. Right now, I'm having trouble straightening my arms because my biceps are still on fire from a WOD (workout of the day) I did two days ago. . I can barely hobble to the men's room without wincing in pain. But, I have a huge smile on my face the entire time. Oh the sweet pain of my CrossFit addiction! I love every bit of it. But why?

Well, let me try to explain how immediately CrossFit impacted my health:

At 40 years old I'm stronger than my 18 year-old self. I can squat more than I did when I played football at Mahopac High School. I can bench more than when I was playing Rugby at Loyola University, Maryland. My cardio is stronger than when I ran a Marathon in my 30's. My range of motion and flexibility has surpassed my mid 20's when I was taking three yoga classes a week. I've seen the light, and its name is CrossFit. While I've been falling in love with this style of workout, I've been spending a great deal of time in the "box" (CrossFit lingo for gym). I've also been watching the owner of my CrossFit affiliate, CrossFit Westchester grow his business at an insane pace. Chris is no meathead gym rat. He has a Bachelor of Arts in Kinesiology from the University of Michigan, but that's not what has impressed me most about Chris. Chris is one of a kind, and he has created a community of one of a kind individuals at CrossFit Westchester. He is insanely knowledgeable about CrossFit. He's whip smart. He's also a stickler for proper form, etiquette, respect, and fun. He's the life force in a gym filled with bigger than life personalities. If you read my blog, you know that Chris is the type of no-nonsense hardcore entrepreneur I love. He's growing his business by following his passion and bringing the thunder on a daily basis.

Please welcome CrossFit Affiliate Head-trainer & Owner Chris Guerrero

Chris Dessi: How did you first get involved in CrossFit?

Chris Guerrero: I've been involved in fitness my whole life. I was training for my middle school sit-up record since I was 8. I've always been into challenging myself physically and went from bodybuilding workouts to circuit training, to mixed martial arts training. In early 2008 I read an article in Muscle & Fitness about CrossFit. I put it off because I didn't want to "get small." A few months later one of my co-workers at JP Morgan suggested I try Cross-Fit, and sent me some youtube links to his brother in law Rob Orlando — one of the CrossFit OGs who made CrossFit what it is today. I was instantly intrigued and went back to that Muscle & Fitness article from a few months back. They had a "hell week" challenge put forth by CrossFit LA. I chose a Monday to start the week long routine and never looked back since.

Chris Dessi: Your gym is thriving. It seems like it's less a gym and more of a flourishing commu-nity of like-minded people. Why do you think this is true with CrossFit?

Chris Guerrero: I truly believe the community, above all, drives the product. It is exactly that, a place where like minded people get together to push themselves past their physical and mental limits. The bond forged through sweat and hard work is almost as strong as any other, in my opinion. I've have made some lifelong friends here.

Chris Dessi: Starting a business is difficult in the office and at home. How much credit do you give to your support system/family for your success? Or have you done it all alone?

Chris Guerrero: From a financial and labor perspective I have done everything alone. In terms of advice, opinions, and decision making, I have had the amazing support of my girlfriend and family from the beginning. I always have the final say in tough decisions but to have the ability to bounce around ideas and always get honest feedback is invaluable, in my opinion.

Chris Dessi: I recently learned about the expansion plans for the gym last week. What was your vision for CrossFit Westchester? Did you have a roadmap? Or are you just following your passion and letting that lead your expansion?

Chris Guerrero: To be honest I don't have a roadmap. I'm just letting what happens happen. The old Spanish phrase, que sera sera (whatever will be, will be). I've never been motivated by money, expansion or anything else. I'm motivated by enjoying what I do and sharing my passion for fitness with others. I come across as hard at times, but I think people know I'm extremely genuine which helps people follow me into the CrossFit abyss.

Chris Dessi: You're very natural and relaxed with the way you interact with your gym members. You also don't take any BS (i. e. people not listening when you're explaining movements, etc.) Does this just come naturally to you, or do you work at it? I guess what I'm asking is — how do you get through a bad day when you have to interact with your clients so intimately all day? Have you ever lost your composure?

Chris Guerrero: Time, time, time. I've grown up so much in the past six years, mainly because I've been forced to in order to survive. One of my strongest suits as a business owner is self-reflection, and knowing where I'm weak and where I'm strong. I've lost my composure many times in the past, and in turn surely lost tons of potential members because of it. The way I look at things is there is no need to dwell in the past. Move forward each day and present the best version of yourself possible.

Chris Dessi: CrossFit athletes are making headlines with some huge endorsement deals etc. You compete at a high level, and we all see you training v-e-r-y hard. Is that the goal (to get paid to compete)? If so — what would be the pinnacle for you?

Chris Guerrero: Money for personal glory has not, and will never motivate me. I think my tenacity comes from not being the most physically gifted, however, the desire to outwork everyone else. I've gotten pretty far in basket-ball and CrossFit from that alone. I'm willing to do what people won't all the time. I'd love to make the CrossFit Games one day in any regard, whether individual or team but I won't let that define me as a person.

Chris Dessi: You have a phenomenal education from a great university (University of Michigan) — how critical has that education been to your success? What do you say to those who say college is a waste of time?

Chris Guerrero: To be honest in this business not much. I think it helped me get my foot in the door in my finance career at different institutions, but I truly think college was a place for me to get my partying out and grow up.

I became a man. I loved every minute of school. if there were one takeaway, it was responsibility and learning to rely on yourself for most things.

Chris Dessi: I know some guys who are born to run businesses. The type of guys that had an army of kids selling lemonade for them by the time they were 10. You're a successful entrepreneur — have you always been inclined to run your own business? Or did it just happen because it was CrossFit? I guess what I'm asking is — if it weren't for CrossFit would you still be a business owner, or would you be sitting in a cubicle somewhere?

Chris Guerrero: I'd probably be hustling doing something else. I can't imagine my entire life being miserable and working for someone else. From a young age, I've always been a business man. I used to run a pretty awesome candy business on my bus in 5-6 grade. The desire to work hard to better yourself and your position has always been enough.

Chris Dessi: Your CrossFit gym has been in business since 2010 — what advice would you give yourself if you could go back in time?

Chris Guerrero: To be more patient, open to suggestions, and less scared to fail. To not be so hard headed and be more friendly and approachable to new clients. I have a thriving business now and had I been the way I am now back then I'd have 500+ members.

Chris Dessi: As a fellow entrepreneur I know that there are high times and very low times. How do you push through the bad times?

Chris Guerrero: Things change and God has a plan. I don't know what the plan is, but I know I have a good heart and am a good person and do a lot to help people. If CrossFit fails, I'll find something else. Since money is not my main source of motivation I think it makes hard times easier for me to get through.

Chris Dessi: What can you point to as your best habits that have led to the success of your business?

Chris Guerrero: Discipline, work ethic, and self-reflection. The discipline to get stuff done no matter how tired I am. The work ethic to understand that being lazy will only affect me and my bottom line. I know I have to be a go-getter. Finally, realizing that I have a staff of people that are much better than me at certain things, and not being scared to admit it and use them where they are strong.

Chris Dessi: You have a great group of people around you. Your Coaches are fantastic. Creme of the crop athletes — but even better people. What hand do you have in that team? Do you work with them — and coach them? Where have you found them, or have they found you?

Chris Guerrero: My coaches are all home grown. They were all members before, and I saw something in them which I liked. I have never, and will never hire a coach outside of our community as I need to thoroughly trust someone and their intentions before allowing them to play such an important role in my business.

Chris Dessi: It seems (to me) as if you're always in the gym. I talk a lot about work/life balance on my blog. I'm curious

— what's your rhythm? What time are you in bed — wake up, etc. ? How long are your workouts?

Chris Guerrero: I'm the first to admit I lack balance for sure and its something I'm working on. I've lost touch with a lot of good people over this. Normally I wake up between 6-8am and am in bed around 11-12. I workout 2-3 hours per day. The workouts for me are not stressful; it's just something that's become part of my everyday life that I feel I must do in order to feel normal, like sleeping and eating.

Chris Dessi: Do you meditate?

Chris Guerrero: Sometimes, but not nearly enough.

Chris Dessi: People define success differently. For instance, wealth, increased free time, lifestyle, social impact. How do you define success?

Chris Guerrero: To me success is based solely on happiness. Most people define it as how much money you have, but the bottom line is, money DOESN'T buy happiness for most people. I'd rather be happy and poor than rich and miserable. I love waking up and doing what I love because I decided I was going to take a chance on myself.

Chris Dessi: Do you consider yourself a success?

Chris Guerrero: I'm successful yes, but not a success just yet. I'm getting started and realizing that I have quite a few things left to do before I'm done with CrossFit.

Chris Dessi: I've been preaching about CrossFit to whoever will listen. But some have replied that they tried it, and have injured themselves. Is injury a necessary evil with CrossFit or are there ways to avoid injury altogether? I guess what I'm asking is — are people just doing it wrong?

CrossFit Westchester

Chris Guerrero: Just like anything else, if you do it wrong you can get hurt. Shitty trainers lead to shitty outcomes. I think consumers need to be more intelligent about where they are shopping for certain things. We have a track record of helping people recover and rehab from injury. I'm confident most anyone who gave CrossFit Westchester a shot for more than 1 class would feel the same way. Maybe CrossFit wouldn't be for them, but they'd agree that "those guys know what they are doing, and I feel safe there."

Chris Dessi: You're offered $5million cash (after taxes). One condition — you can never do CrossFit ever again. Do you take the money?

Chris Guerrero: Not a chance. My freedom and happiness don't have a price.

SPEED ROUND

Chris Dessi: Last thing you bought?

Chris Guerrero: Lokai Bracelet

Chris Dessi: Last person you argued with?

Chris Guerrero: My Girlfriend

Chris Dessi: One of your stuffed animals' names as a kid?

Chris Guerrero: Honestly I only remember one, which was the Flounder from the Little Mermaid

Chris Dessi: Favorite day of the week?

Chris Guerrero: Monday

Chris Dessi: Favorite curse word?

Chris Guerrero: Fuck — I curse way too much

Chris Dessi: Do you play a musical instrument?

Chris Guerrero: No

Chris Dessi: T. V. show you secretly enjoy?

Chris Guerrero: Alaskan Bush People and most things Discovery

Chris Dessi: One place you could travel right now?

Chris Guerrero: Hawaii

Chris Dessi: Who is the first person you call when things go wrong in your day?

Chris Guerrero: Either my mom or my girlfriend

Chris Dessi: Mets or Yankees?

Chris Guerrero: Yankees but I don't really like baseball

Chris Dessi: Favorite band?

Chris Guerrero: N/A — very close minded with music

Chris Dessi: Rap or Rock?

Chris Guerrero: Rap

To learn more about how you can join CrossFit Westchester visit http://crossfitwestchester.com/

The Transformative
Powerof Focus

SHEILA HAILE
Chief Marketing Officer at Cohen's Fashion Optical

I love what I do. I love it even more when I'm inspired by the people that surround me. I met Sheila Haile, Chief Marketing Officer at Cohen's Fashion Optical, only a few months ago. I enjoy collaborating with Sheila immensely. I find myself learning from her, and that's thrilling. She's that rare combination of personality and intellect. A true joy to be around. We both share an insane work ethic — many times exchanging work emails on Sundays.

Innovation and creativity inspire Sheila, and I'm inspired to meet her lofty goals.

She does it ALL. She's a mother of two great kids and CMO at Cohen's. We all know how difficult it is to juggle career and family, but Sheila makes it look effortless. She's responsible for Print, TV, digital, video, mobile, experiential, PR, content marketing, SEO, search, PPC, local search, visual merchandising, and,

Sheila's Family

of course, social media. Yowza. She's been able to excel in so many facets of her life. I believe that *laser focus* is her secret. People like Sheila fascinate me. I think she'll fascinate you too.

Here we go.

Chris Dessi: We've only known each other for a short time, but you're a powerhouse. Wife, kids, CMO — how do you find the time to do it all? I guess another way of saying it is — what's your rhythm? When do you go to bed, work out, wake up?

Sheila & Family

Sheila Haile: I am a morning person. I got into the habit when the kids were little and I needed to carve out some time to clear my head. I have no interest in being the last person at the party!

Chris Dessi: You've had a storied career, winning all sorts of accolades. 2012 Most Influential Women in Optical — too many MarComm awards to list. When did you first consider yourself a success?

Sheila Haile: That thought does not even cross my mind. I don't believe you are a success until there is nothing left to do. And there is so much more I want to do, in all phases of my life. I don't feel like I've accomplished the big one yet.

Chris Dessi: We regularly exchange emails late at night and on Sundays. You seem to have one gear "HARD WORK." What motivates you to work so hard?

Sheila Haile: I love what I do. I love the energy, the creativity and the opportunity to create and build something. The end product motivates me...

Chris Dessi: What impact, if any has web 2. 0 /social media had on your personal success?

Sheila Haile: I don't know any different. I don't consider myself a tech head...I just use the tools available the best ways possible.

Chris Dessi: You're a triathlete. How did you first get involved in the sport?

Sheila Haile: I was a college swimmer and runner. I started to run competitively again when my oldest was very little as an outlet and a way to meet people in a new area. I joined a running group...and was introduced to people similar to me. I actually met my best friend in that first group. The running group introduced me to triathlon and I immediate loved it. It was a great sport for many, many years.

I don't consider myself a triathlete anymore. For me, it was a unique phase of my life that functioned almost like therapy. It allowed me to focus and clear my head. I made a conscience decision to pull away from the lifestyle. I knew I couldn't do it all. As my kids grew up, I needed to focus on them. It was their time to shine in their sports. I got much more satisfaction watching them succeed than I ever did on my own.

Chris Dessi: Are there characteristics that have helped you in business that you honed as a tri-athlete?

Sheila Haile: Focus.commitment. Time management!

Chris Dessi: Speaking of your health — how important is maintaining your health to your success— spiritual and phys-ical? Do you attend church? Meditate? Workout regularly?

Sheila Haile: Health is incredibly important to me. For many layered and deep reasons. I lost my mother at a young age. The early loss of my mother has a very strong impact on who I became. At a very early age, I had to rely on myself. My career was just beginning I didn't even have anyone to ask what to wear to an interview. I had to figure it out pretty quick. That experience taught me that we have to take care of ourselves. I have had some very difficult medical struggles of my own that have had a lasting impact on me as well.

These obstacles shape who you are. They truly make a person understand what matters in life. For me, they made my drive sharper and the incredible need for balance even more strong. I vowed to be the best mother I could be while growing my career at the same time. Not always easy and I often behaved like a maniac to achieve it.

Fitness helped me through some difficult times. Health struggles of my own that I needed to "work out". But, it can go too far as well. I was training for a half ironman when Cole was three and Nick was in 2nd grade .... a doozer of an event: 1. 5 mile swim, 60 mile bike, and 13 mile run...when I took a major spill. About two weeks before the event, and after six months of training...I was out. What a life lesson. I smashed half my body, broke my elbow in a million pieces, got a soft tissue injury on my hip. I was in the hospital, had surgery and had a cast for several weeks. I rolled the boys around town in a red wagon because I couldn't drive.

Game changer. The accident taught me I couldn't do it all. I was lucky to be alive. I realized I had to make some choices.

Chris Dessi: What was the single most important decision you made that contributed to your success?

Sheila Haile: Committing to what I loved. I was the weird art kid. But I knew who I was, and I was "allowed" to embrace it. I went to Wesleyan University at 16 to study all aspects of art, design, dance and theater. I studied abroad in Italy and traveled extensively. I learn by experience. These things made me who I am.

Chris Dessi: How do you define success?

Sheila Haile: When you have reached a pinnacle of what you set out to do that you can begin to teach others. I am not there yet.

Chris Dessi: You're a woman in business, and you're excelling. What's the best piece of advice you can offer young women starting out in business?

Sheila Haile: Life is about balance. Be honest with who you are and what you want, then build around that. The two best pieces of advise I have ever gotten more as a mother than a woman in business:

You can do it all …just not at the same time. You don't get a do-over when raising your kids.

Chris Dessi: Who have you looked to you in your career as a mentor?

Sheila Haile: I don't have a single mentor. Know anyone? I would love a mentor!

Chris Dessi: You have a degree from Manhattanville College, I'm curious: how important has education been to your success? What do you say to those that say a college education isn't worth it?

Sheila Haile: Education and exposure are critical to growth. Experiencing life and seeing cultures of all kinds can broaden your view.

College education is absolutely worth it. Education exposes your mind to new ways of thinking. I love school and have been taking classes and going to seminars consistently for many years. College is the time for you to become yourself.

Chris Dessi: If you could travel in time and speak with the 22 year-old Sheila Hale — what is the one piece of advice you'd give her?

Sheila Haile: Go a little easier on yourself.

Chris Dessi: How do you deal with adversity and setbacks?

Sheila Haile: With each set back there is a takeaway. I try

to look at it objectively and see how I screwed up and what I could have done better. I truly believe that you learn more from a mistake than by doing everything right.

Adversity is a different ballgame. Being in an unbalanced situation is the most difficult for me.

Chris Dessi: You have laser focus, but you also know when to relax. I think that's why we get along so well, how do you strike that ever elusive work/life balance? Especially with a husband and children at home?

I'm all about the balance. Everyone's balance is different. My kids always came first. Period. I did not miss an event, play or game. Even if I was running across the field as the starting gun went off. (Happened more than once). I knew each event for them was "the big one"…and I was there when they looked up in the stands. I could and would work all night if I had to, to make up for it. I wanted to make it work because I loved what I did.

Chris Dessi: What do you think has separated you from other high performers throughout your career?

Sheila Haile: You have to put in the work every day, just like everyone else. I am no better than the next guy.

Chris Dessi: I know you as a very humble person — but now is your time to brag. Tell me about some of your biggest wins.

Sheila Haile: My kids are big wins. To watch them become adults is the most extraordinary experience. It really does work! I have had some nice wins in pitching on the agency side and some nice opportunities to be recognized by my peers. Always nice.

RAPID FIRE

Chris Dessi: Have you ever had a nickname? What is it?

Sheila Haile: She-She. My godchild used to call me that when she was little.

Chris Dessi: My daughters know that I hate witches — what's one thing that scares the hell out of you?

Sheila Haile: Heights.

Chris Dessi: Best day of your life:

Sheila Haile: 2 of them: when the kids were born.

Chris Dessi: Worst day of your life?

Sheila Haile: I lost some important people in my life. Those were difficult times.

Chris Dessi: What is the best gift you have been given?

Sheila Haile: My kids

Chris Dessi: You have access to a time machine, but you can never come back to present day. You can go into the future, or into the past. Where do you go in time?

Sheila Haile: I would go to the future, but everyone I care about has to come too.

Chris Dessi: Who is your hero?

Sheila Haile: No heros. There are people I think are extraordinary...very varied...from Georgia O Keefe to Oprah. . but I don't have a hero.

Chris Dessi: Name someone who knows more about you than anyone else in the world.

Sheila Haile: My husband.

Chris Dessi: If you could share a meal with any four individuals, living or dead, who would they be?

Sheila Haile: Me, my mother, and my boys and my husband.

Chris Dessi: Most powerful business book you've ever read that you recommend to everyone.

Sheila Haile: I read a lot, but I don't have a business book that changed my life, but many other books life made an incredible impact on my thinking.

Chris Dessi: If you were a superhero, what powers would you have?

Sheila Haile: Happiness. All the time.

A New World Success Forged by Old World Expertise

JOHN HALL, CEO, Influence & CO. #72 FORBES'
"America's Most Promising Companies"

John Hall is one of the most powerful people in media who you've *never* met. He's the mastermind behind Influence and Co. Forbes recently listed them as one of "America's Most Promising Companies." If you want to be a thought leader, John is the gatekeeper. When meeting John in person, you'd never know the power this one man can wield. He's filled with humility and charming reverence. Get him on a stage, and he will rock you to the core. John and his team are at the tip of the "thought leader" wave. Surfing the edge where the crest of the new and compelling is just breaking, crashing down on the old, and dusty. They are trailblazers. John has been a speaker at two <u>Westchester Digital Summit's</u>. He's an impressive executive for sure. He's an even more impressive person. Balancing a start-up that is exploding on the scene, traveling the country speaking, and raising a brand new baby at home. Forbes says Influence & Co, is "one of the largest suppliers of expert content to media outlets." The publication recently named John as one of the <u>10 Keynote Speakers Who Will Keep You Ahead of Digital Marketing Trends</u>. There's a new world order, and it looks like John Hall. I'm honored to welcome him to the pages of my book.

Chris Dessi: You're a father, a CEO, and you have a weekly column at Forbes and Inc.com. Where do you find the time? What's your rhythm? When do you go to bed, work out, wake up?

John Hall: I typically work from home from 8 to 10 in the morning, and then I head to the office. I work there until 5 when I head home to spend time with my family and play with my daughter. I try to get more work done around 8 in the evening, and I get to sleep around 11 p. m.

Chris Dessi: You've been at the helm of <u>Influence & Co</u>. for four years now. You're still a young man, but you're an obvious success. When did you first consider yourself a success?

John Hall: I'm still working on it. I look at my success in several different areas and continuously grade myself on what I can do better. Nobody's perfect, and there's always going to be something you can do better.

We all have different perceptions of success and ways to measure how we're living up to the success we desire for ourselves. I recently wrote an article about success for Forbes, and in it, I talk about seven main standards of success I believe every leader should strive to excel at. I regularly grade myself in each of these areas to hold myself accountable and strive for personal success.

Chris Dessi: What mindset helps to make you successful?

John Hall: The most successful people I know don't act like they've got it all figured out. They have the mindset that it's OK to admit you could have handled something differently and that you can always improve. Having a mindset like that is very helpful.

Chris Dessi: What is the greatest accomplishment of your life?

John Hall: Being a father to my daughter has been the greatest accomplishment of my life.

Chris Dessi: How do you define success?

John Hall: I get more in-depth about this in my Forbes article that I mentioned above, but I use seven key standards to measure myself and my success. I believe that being successful means having a healthy relationship with yourself where you challenge yourself personally and professionally, but you also realize that you're not perfect.

Success means having a gratifying family life in which you treat the people who are most important to you like they're most important to you. It means being financially comfortable and in good mental and physical health. Success is having a fulfilling career and career path, genuine respect for others, and general contentment with your lifestyle.

Chris Dessi: What impact, if any, has Web 2. 0 had on your success? To put it another way, would Influence & Co. be successful without social media?

John Hall: Social media is one of the biggest amplifiers of content, and it certainly is a piece of our success, but Influence & Co. would still be successful without it. The expertise that exists within a company and its leaders are extremely valuable, and creating content from that expertise that can be distributed to the right audience is vital. Producing and distributing that content would still be important with our without social media.

Chris Dessi: How important is it for executives (no matter what level) to have a thriving personal digital brand identity? Students? Entrepreneurs?

John Hall: A strong brand identity is important for each of the above. Your brand identity is one of your greatest assets, and it's what will drive opportunities to you and to the company you represent. As long as you build and maintain a strong, positive brand for yourself, there will always be opportunities for you — whether you're an experienced executive, an entrepreneur getting your business off the ground, or a student just starting out.

Chris Dessi: I love reading all of the content you generate. It's high quality, informative, and not sales heavy. How important is it for other CEOs to follow your lead and generate valuable content in their industries? Can they survive in our modern era without being content publishers?

John Hall: If you don't want to give yourself or your company a competitive advantage, then don't worry about creating content; I'm sure some companies could survive without becoming a content creator and publisher. However, it's become such an essential part of differentiating your company and leading your industry that I'd highly recommend all business leaders generate valuable thought leadership content.

People want a human connection with a company. They need to trust you and trust your brand, and one of the best ways they can do that is through reading your content. I can tell you from my personal experience that business opportunities consistently come to us at Influence & Co. through my published content. And it not only brings us opportunities, but it makes me a better leader by challenging me to stay ahead of the game.

Chris Dessi: If a crystal ball could tell you the truth about yourself, your life, the future, or anything else, what would you want to know?

John Hall: I wouldn't want to know anything. I like to experience life as it's thrown at me.

Chris Dessi: If you could change anything about the way you were raised, what would it be?

John Hall: I wouldn't change a thing. I was blessed to have great parents.

Chris Dessi: How important is maintaining your health to your success — spiritual and physical? Do you attend church? Meditate? Work out regularly?

John Hall: Maintaining good health is one of the metrics

I use in my personal definition of success. It's such a huge part of success because it affects every other metric. Without it, success becomes much harder to achieve in the other areas I've set for myself.

To maintain my health, I work out pretty regularly and set goals for myself. One of the best things you can do for your health is just to be aware of it. Be proactive. Realize that you need to take care of yourself, and take the right steps to make that happen.

I recently got a blood test and a few other tests after I turned 30, and it gave me great insight into where I was physically and where I needed to improve. It had taken me so long to get around to actually having it done because I was always "so busy," but in reality, nothing should keep you so busy that you can't stay healthy.

Chris Dessi: What was the single most import-ant decision you made that contributed to your success?

John Hall: At a young age, I decided that I would take my personal finance seriously. I got on top of my game and was able to buy real estate at age 19. It allowed me to build my first company. That financial security put me on track to afford to do a lot of things that  I wanted to do rather than what I had to do, and that independence has contributed greatly to my success.

Chris Dessi: Your clients are very influential people across multiple industries. What is the one trait they all possess that has made them so successful?

John Hall: Our best clients are the ones who truly *care about the people in their target audiences*. They care about their customers, and they want to give as much value to them as possible. They say things like, "We have real expertise that we need to share with this audience. We have experience and knowledge that can help them." That's what our clients have in common. The worst kind of clients, the kind we try not to take on, are the ones who only care about their egos. They're only in it for themselves or the numbers. That's so radically different from what our best clients are like.

Chris Dessi: Who have you looked to as a mentor in your career?

John Hall: I don't have any one mentor. I look to a variety of people, like my parents, close friends, and co-workers. I think it's important to surround yourself with good people, people you admire and respect, and pay attention to the things they do that you like and don't like. Just paying attention to the people you respect helps you learn so much about how you want to be.

Chris Dessi: You have a Master's in Accounting from the University of Missouri—Columbia. I'm curious: How important has education been to your success? What do you say to those who say a college education isn't worth it?

John Hall: I don't think I'd say my education has been that important to my success. College gave me a chance to learn things like communication, relationship management, and problem solving skills, but a lot of that came just by being involved in various organizations or through internships throughout college. I think a college education is worth getting, but I absolutely recommend that a student supplements her coursework with as many real-world experiences and opportunities to build herself as an asset to her fields as she can find. Do everything you can to gain experience that's relevant to your industry.

Chris Dessi: How do you deal with adversity and setbacks?

John Hall: Head-on. It's easy to sweep things under the rug and to avoid the things that make you uncomfortable. As I've gotten older, I've learned that adversity makes you stronger, and now I look forward to my chances to overcome my setbacks, learn more about myself, and grow stronger.

Chris Dessi: We've hosted you as a speaker two years in a row at the Westchester Digital Summit. When most people would rather be dead than be the person delivering the eulogy, how do you do it? Does public speaking come naturally to you? To put it another  way, what are some tips you have for my readers to help them deliver a John Hall caliber address at their next conference?

John Hall: The truth is, I still get nervous before most speeches. Preparation helps ease my nerves, but my best advice is just to have a conversation with your audience. Try not to look at the group as an entire group. Look at individuals in that group. Just look at them like you would if you were having a casual drink with them.

Chris Dessi: I know you as a very humble person, but now is your time to brag. Tell me about some of your biggest wins.

John Hall: I'm really proud of having a great little family and a thriving company. I'm writing these answers as I'm taking my family to Disney World. The fact that I have this beautiful family and that we can take trips like this together is a huge win. It's great to be able to separate from work every once in a while and have this special time.

It's also been exciting to see Influence & Co. grow and receive awards. We made Forbes' "Most Promising Companies" list and were recognized at the United Nations for Best Marketing Company in 2014, and both of those wins were nice for us. However, most of these types of wins are team wins and not just my wins.

RAPID FIRE

Chris Dessi: Have you ever had a nickname? What is it?

John Hall: Nope. Just John. Sorry, I'm not interesting there.

Chris Dessi: My daughters know that I hate witches. What's one thing that scares the hell out of you?

John Hall: Failure. I've been blessed not to have a lot of serious failures yet, so I'm scared of something happening at this point that would cause me to lose everything I've worked so hard for.

Chris Dessi: What's been the best day of your life?

John Hall: Hands down, the day my daughter was born.

Chris Dessi: Worst?

John Hall: The day my friend got shot and murdered at a party in college.

Chris Dessi: What's your favorite holiday?

John Hall: Christmas.

Chris Dessi: What was the last book you read?

John Hall: I can't remember.

Chris Dessi: Who's your hero?

John Hall: I have a lot of heroes.

Chris Dessi: Are you a clean or messy person?

John Hall: In between, but leaning toward messy.

Chris Dessi: Who would you want to play you in a movie of your life?

John Hall: Ryan Reynolds. I'd say the looks might be slightly misleading, but I'm OK with that.

Chris Dessi: Do you love or hate rollercoasters?

John Hall: I'm scared of heights and haven't ridden a rollercoaster for a while, but I used to love them.

Chris Dessi: What's your favorite movie?

John Hall: Growing up, my favorite was "The Secret of my Success." Now it's got to be "Frozen" because I have to watch it at least once a day.

Chris Dessi: What was your favorite subject in school?

John Hall: Math.

An Exclusive Look into the Success of TV Journalist Chris Hansen

CHRIS HANSEN
TV Journalist & Author

The story went something like this: He was in a desert. The details are a bit fuzzy. He may have been with guides taking him to see a drug lord. Or he was with government operatives. I forget. But, they were in a desert, and it was a dangerous scenario. What I do remember is him telling me what they saw. They stumbled upon a rattlesnake. His imitation of the rattlesnake threw me. It was pitch perfect. He said he froze with fear. I froze too. Jaw dropped. Riveted. In my mind, I was there in the desert with him. Confronted by that rattlesnake. He drew me into his story. That *voice*. That Chris Hansen voice. The familiar voice we all know. He took me to that moment. In reality, I was sitting across from Chris in a restaurant in Stamford, CT. But he took me there with him, into the desert. I was staring down a rattlesnake. What is it about *this* guy? The intense eye contact? The delivery? The voice. Yep. That's it, I thought. It's his VOICE that gets you. Plus his delivery. The drawn out words. The dramaaaaaatic presentation. Knowing just where to addddddd inflection. When to float a sentence in a loooooooow baritone. Peak an inquiry with a touch of knowing midwestern charm. I thought to myself "this guy is special."

We all know the lines we can recite by heart. "What is it exactly that you were planning on doing here today?" Even more popular, "Why don't you have a seat right over there." He's transcended journalism. He now resides in that ever elusive place within the American psyche. He's part of our pop culture. There are so many vacuous & talentless people who reside in that space. You tend to lump them in the same talentless

category. Sometimes you forget that others landed there because of their prodigious talent. That's what he is. A prodigious talent. He had me. Sitting there in a restaurant in Stamford, CT. I was putty in his hands. He could have told me anything, and I would have believed him intrinsically. I would have admitted anything to him. I had to snap myself out of it. "Holy shit, Chris that's the best story I've ever heard in my life." He chuckled, but he didn't stop me from gushing. He knows he's good at this. He alluded to his power to elicit a confession from anyone he encounters. Here he shifts gears and shares a story about his son. Something about how his son attempted to fib to him about a stolen bottle of booze from the family liquor cabinet. Standard teenage high-jinx. But when your Dad is Chris Hansen? Nothing standard about that interrogation. I find myself feeling compassion for his son. Poor kid didn't stand a chance!

Is it just his voice? That's part of it for sure. Maybe it was the years of experience as a journalist. Knowing what combination of voice + inflection + plus pregnant pause will make people lean in. The lead in for his story while we were sitting at that table sounded scripted. It sounded like it should have been a voiceover to a special mini-series. I felt transported. He is the best storyteller I've ever met. Ever.

Chris Hansen is many things. A cultural icon. An award-winning journalist. For sure. He's also a decent guy and an infinitely curious guy. I admire curiosity. I admire people who stay in motion. Those who don't rest. On either laurels or reputation. That's not Chris. He's a land shark. Always moving so he can breathe.

He's an old school guy with infinite respect for the new school. It's the reason he will remain relevant in our culture for years to come.

Chris Hansen is a global star. Chris Hansen is a huge success. He's interviewed so many people. I consider it a huge honor to interview someone of Chris' caliber.

Let's do this:

Chris Dessi: You've had a storied career. You're an international celebrity. How does a kid from Bloomfield Hill, Michigan get here? What has your journey been like? What were the ups and downs?

Chris Hansen: I always joke that I am too stupid to realize there's anything I cannot do. I guess I have never put limits on myself and when it comes to potential show or story ideas, I have always listened to people…whether it's a train conductor, a cop or a CEO, everyone has a story. I embraced the business early on. When I was 14, Jimmy Hoffa was kidnapped from a restaurant up the street from my house. I was fascinated by the crime and the media coverage. The news bug bit me. I have had many more ups than downs and more lucky breaks than one guy deserves, but from Lansing to Tampa to Detroit to New York, I have always tried to be the hardest working guy on the team.

Chris Dessi: Over lunch you once mentioned to me that you didn't wear a tie on the set of "To Catch a Predator." You explained that you were concerned that one of the perpetrators may grab you by your tie. I found this fascinating, but it also begs the question — have you ever been afraid for your life while working on a story?

Chris Hansen: True! As part of our security protocol, I didn't want one of the predators to be able to grab my tie and drag me across the counter. I was in that situation once in a bar fight in Detroit… always kind of stuck with me. It's why cops wear clip-ons. Also, a tie just felt a little formal in that kind of a situation. Have I ever been scared? Of course! No one actually tried to hurt me during the predator investigations, but you never know what someone is capable of. 300 predators and not a scratch, but interview a guy selling counterfeit Mophies in a Connecticut mall and I almost  get my ass kicked. We did have a guy an off-duty cop, actually show up after we had shut down the predator house for the night. Police pulled him over; he had four guns and hundreds of rounds of ammo in his car. Who know what could have happened had he come into the house when we were there. Flying with the Mexican federal place on a raid looking for a cartel leader was a bit scary, but most because we were in an overloaded 727 built in 1966. Truth is, overseas, the scariest thing to me is getting into a traffic accident.

Chris Dessi: Many people have the intellect. Many more have the looks. What is it that has separated you from the crowd? I guess what I'm trying to say is — what one skill or trait do you feel has contributed most to the success you've seen in your life?

Chris Hansen: Looks don't hurt, but I think it's my voice that is most distinctive. You need to separate yourself from the crowd. I do it with my interview style. I listen. I don't look at a question list. I get into someone's mind. If I am exhausted after an interview, I know I have done a good job.

Chris Dessi: We've joked about your perfectly quaffed hair. You're a handsome guy. Looks are part of the job — but how do you react to some anchors that look more like models than journalists?

Chris Hansen: I'd rather watch someone who is interesting and knows what they are talking about than a former model. I don't think viewers demand movie star looks. You do need to take care of yourself and present well. It's like being a CEO. You represent the brand, the network, and your product.

Chris Dessi: You've interviewed some dangerous people — pedophiles, drug lords, corrupt politicians. Has any of them surprised you? Like, have you thought to yourself "Boy, if this guy went another direction we could have been pals."

Chris Hansen: Sure. There are some charming inmates in prison. It always fascinates me how the random twists and turns in life can make someone a criminal or a victim. It's also interesting to me how, if a criminal had turned their energy towards something positive, they could have been a success.

Chris Dessi: You've traveled the world, and had the opportunity to meet many people. Do you find that the successful people you've encountered share the same traits? If so, what are they? Or is it one thing only?

Chris Hansen: It's many things, but more than anything else it's passion for a cause, for success, passion is the key. You need to like and believe in what you are doing. You also have to con-vince others to support you and believe in you.

Chris Dessi: Who has been the most fascinating person

you've ever interviewed, and why?

Chris Hansen: The most fascinating person? That's a tough one. Colin Powell for a big investigation on child sex trafficking. One of the most compelling though was the interview I did with all 12 jurors in the Timothy Mcveigh case. They had just convicted him and cleared the way for his execution in the Oklahoma City bombing case.

Chris Dessi: When was the first time you took a step back and said "yeah, I've made it." You're famous. You've seen monetary reward for your work. You've won SEVEN Emmy Awards. That list equates to the definition of success in our society. How do you define success? Has the fame, money, and awards, ever clouded that definition?

Chris Hansen: I am still trying to "make it" but I think being stopped on the street or in an airport or restaurant by someone who saw one of my shows. My sons have always had a father on TV, so it's no big deal for them, but when i was parodied on South Park, suddenly I had made it in their eyes and just for the record it's EIGHT Emmys! My definition of success is that I get to do what I really love and I actually get paid for it. 34 years into the business and I still love it, still love the competition and the drive the stay ahead of the quickly evolving nature of what I do and how I do it.

Chris Dessi: What's your rhythm? Do you work out? What time are you in bed/wake up? Do you meditate?

Chris Hansen: I am usually an early riser. I have a personal trainer and when I am not traveling, I usually workout with her 90 minutes four days a week. On the road, I run or hit the gym. Skiing is meditation to me and an hour a week one on one with the tennis pro is cheaper than therapy.

Chris Dessi: You've participated in my even the Westchester Digital Summit two years in a row. You know that our world is changing rapidly with the advent of social media, and you've embraced it. More recently, you have been leveraging it to great success. As I write this, you've crowdsourced 1,220 backers pledged $89,068 to help bring your "Hansen vs. Predator" project to life. How important has being able to adapt and roll with big change been in your career? Or is this a trait that you're just embracing now?

Chris Hansen: The Westchester Digital Summit is a prime example of how I try to keep up with the explosive changes in all media, especially digital. Whether it's my Kickstarter campaign or doing a Reddit AMA to promote a new show, you have to stay on top of all this. I do it my surrounding myself with smart young people.

Chris Dessi: There have been times in your life when the grumbling under-belly of the media world have aggres-sively and unfairly targeted you, your  family and your personal life. How important has having a thick skin been to your success?

Chris Hansen: I'm sorry did you say something? Ha. Anyone can be a blogger these days and say whatever they want about you at any time. They don't have to follow the rules I follow. When I write something about someone, I talk to them to get their side of the story. That basic fundamental fairness has been lost in many corners of digital media. Thick skin? Look, if you play in the NFL, you are going to take some hits and some cheap shots.

Chris Dessi: Dealing with that couldn't have been an easy time in your life, but you're in the midst of an epic comeback. What has helped you get through the dark times? Who do you turn to when things get rocky?

Chris Hansen: There have been no dark times. It takes time to ramp up new projects. Longer than I thought? sure. Worth the extra effort? Absolutely.

Chris Dessi: Have you ever had a mentor? How important do you think mentorship is for the success of young people?

Chris Hansen: I am very fortunate to have strong mentors. Anchormen Bill Bonds in Detroit from the age of 16 and Howard Lancour in Lansing most notably. Wouldn't be where I am without them.

Chris Dessi: What is the on-air moment you're most proud of?

Chris Hansen: The proudest moment on air is when everyone at NBC during 911 managed to keep their composure and report under some of the most difficult circumstances imaginable. It wasn't work; it was a mission.

Chris Dessi: What do you think your 12 year-old self would say to you today?

Chris Hansen: Cool car man! 2014 Corvette. Still just a motorhead from Detroit.

Chris Dessi: You're a recognizable guy around the globe. What's the oddest place someone has recognized you?

Chris Hansen: Cheng Mai, Thailand. An American in a hotel recognized me and broke into a sweat. While he wasn't the target of our investigation, I suspect he was up to no good.

Chris Dessi: You have a degree from Michigan State. What do you say to those who believe that college is a waste of money?

Chris Hansen: Go to college, though I think many would be served better by two years of community college and work before going to University. More affordable and a lot of kids would be more focused.

SPEED ROUND

Chris Dessi: Dan Rather or Peter Jennings?

Chris Hansen: Jennings

Chris Dessi: Best journalist you've ever met?

Chris Hansen: Mike Wallace

Chris Dessi: What five words would your children use to describe you?

Chris Hansen: My dad is Chris Hansen

Chris Dessi: Favorite movie?

Chris Hansen: North By Northwest

Chris Dessi: Who is your hero?

Chris Hansen: Tom Brokaw

Chris Dessi: Funniest person you know?

Chris Hansen: Dan Dietz

Chris Dessi: Worst day of your life?

Chris Hansen: The day my Father passed away.

Chris Dessi: Best day of your life?

Chris Hansen: When my sons were born.

Chris Dessi: Who should play you in a movie?

Chris Hansen: Bradley Cooper or Dennis Leary

Chris Dessi: What is your favorite word?

Chris Hansen: "Explain"

To learn more about Chris follow him on Twitter:
https://twitter.com/chrishansen

and

Killer Instinct with Chris Hansen MONDAY 10/9C

Success Tips From a CEO, Best Selling Author, and Television Celebrity

JEFFREY HAYZLETT
Primetime TV & Radio Host, Keynote Speaker, Best-Selling Author, and Global Business Celebrity

As I write this, Jeffrey Hayzlett is a best-selling author, a primetime TV host, radio host, runs a PR firm and is a former CMO of a Fortune 500 company. What's more, I don't see him slowing down anytime soon. My business partner John Zanzarella and I love Jeffrey Hayzlett. John and I have taken a few meetings with Jeffrey, and we always leave the room smarter than when we entered. Jeffrey is a high octane, move a million miles an hour, *business cowboy*, with a shotgun slung over his shoulder. The guy is all straight talk. All passion. No frills perfection. In a world of tip toe on eggshells political correctness, Jeffrey calls it how he sees it — because he can. Which is why he was an obvious choice for John and me to have him keynote the Westchester Digital Summit. Jeffrey blew the roof off our event. He was recently inducted into the speaker's Hall of Fame. Oh yeah — he's also a newly minted grandfather. Let's welcome Jeffrey to the Success feature, because — hell, this guy deserves it!

Wait.

Let me stop myself.

I feel like I'm a gameshow host introducing one of the spokesmodels. Ok — here's the real deal. When I first met Jeffrey he *scared the shit out of me*. When he walked in, I said to myself "shit — that's a big dude." His right hand is bigger than my head. He had just gotten back from a TV appearance defending the bad behavior of Alex Baldwin. Yep — DEFENDING.

Oof.

I didn't know what to make of him. But, since that first meeting Jeffrey has collaborated with our team and helped us greatly. His insight, participation, and guidance has been invaluable to my agency as we deal with astronomical growing pains. His keynote was a highlight at the summit. While Jeffrey was speaking, I was in a side room interviewing our Westchester County Executive — Rob Astorino. We had to keep stopping the interview because Jeffrey's voice was bellowing throughout the conference hall. The crowd was eating it up. This is a guy who's seen it all in the C-suite, but he's humble enough to know that he had to reinvent himself to remain a success. Jeffrey is currently on a book tour sharing his insights from his business back stories and sharing examples from the many business leaders he's worked with throughout his career. He's a touch of old school, a dab of new school and a ton of bravado. Just the way I like it.

There, I feel better — let's do this.

Chris Dessi: You're at a cocktail party, and one of your contemporaries says something like "I don't get that Twitter thing — I don't care about what you had for lunch"… how do you respond to them? I guess what I'm asking is — how do you explain the power of social media to someone who dismisses it?

Jeffrey Hayzlett: My first response would be something very direct like, 'you have to be an idiot not to be using social media." And after they spit out their cocktail, I would then proceed to explain the benefits of social engagement and building brand ambassadors for your brand. This is the new way of selling. I'm using Twitter, Facebook, LinkedIn, Instagram, to not only engage audiences but to sell products. Business leaders need to understand that their community is online, and if you want to reach them, you need to be there, too. That's what social media is about, engaging with an audience that is interested in your company.

Chris Dessi: What the hell is it about bacon that has you so enamored? Why not devil dogs, or lollipops, or hamburgers? What do you think it is about bacon?

Jeffrey Hayzlett: Duh, because it's bacon! Don't make fun of bacon; I'll have to hurt you. Seriously, everything goes better with bacon. You can even eat Brussels Sprouts with bacon on it! Although, if I were you I would just throw out the Brussels Sprouts and just eat the bacon. I mean, why go through all that hassle when you can just eat bacon?

Chris Dessi: Many people would consider themselves a success if they accomplished just one of your many accomplishments (write a book, appear on TV, etc.). When did you first consider yourself a success?

Jeffrey Hayzlett: I don't know if I have ever looked at it like that. I was brought up to believe that no matter what you did, as long as you did it right, you are a success. That's the way I approach things in life and if I can add zeros onto it well, then, that makes me wealthy and smart. Don't get me wrong; I'm not always successful, but usually that's just timing.

Chris Dessi: How do you define success?

Jeffrey Hayzlett: I think all things around success are defined by mutual conditions of satisfaction. Everyone needs to have a sense of what their conditions of satisfaction are. For me, it's about building wealth, having fun and learning something new.

Chris Dessi: You recently delivered a powerful keynote at my event, the Westchester Digital Summit. Does that come naturally, or have you worked on your presentation skills?

Jeffrey Hayzlett: I think it's easier for some people rather than others. Some people just have a natural ability to connect with audiences. That being said, one needs to practice and prepare. Just like in sales or anything else it's called hard work because it's hard. A good practitioner is always honing their craft, finding the perfect timing or the right story, so the audience gets the most of their experience.

Chris Dessi: What advice can you give my readers who want to be successful public speakers like yourself?

Jeffrey Hayzlett: The biggest free advice I can give is to practice, practice, practice. This can be applied to any job, task or profession. My second piece of advice is to watch those who are the very best at their craft. Not to steal their ideas. If you're stealing ideas, you're only cheating yourself. Learn how the masters work. I was recently inducted into the speaker's Hall of Fame, and I am now listed among some of the greatest speakers in the world. I grew up watching and learning from those speakers. My last piece of advice is to be genuine. You can tell a great and authentic speaker because it just oozes out of every word, every movement, every story and that's what helps make them great. Being in business can be tough.

Chris Dessi: You've enjoyed some good times, but I think that's boring. I'm more interested in learning how you push through your worst times?

Jeffrey Hayzlett: I've mentioned earlier that it's called hard work because it's hard. It's not easy to be in business for yourself or in any business for that matter. It's not the lucky who win, but the relentless that succeed in the end. Never be afraid of hard times, because in your career you'll face numerous hard times. The key is to realize what's coming and always be ready to handle the toughest situations. That way when times are good you will succeed faster.

Chris Dessi: Which habit has helped yield the most success for you? What I mean is — are you an obsessive networker, or cold caller?

Jeffrey Hayzlett: I use both, but I'm a bigger networker than I am a cold caller. Not that I like one over the other, but I've found that by being a really great networker, I don't have to make as many cold calls because people call me.

Chris Dessi: Do you watch a lot of TV? If so, what's your favorite show?

Jeffrey Hayzlett: I don't watch as much TV as I used to but when I do watch I like shows where I learn things, like Antique Roadshow. Although, I have to admit I'm a fan of The Big Bang Theory it's so well written, and it makes me laugh.

Chris Dessi: What's your rhythm? How much sleep do you need? What time are you in bed/up in the morning?

Jeffrey Hayzlett: I can get by with about five hours of sleep a night. I tend to go to bed very late and wake up early. However, I do like to sleep in every so often. Every three or four months I catch up by sleeping in very late

Chris Dessi: Do you exercise? Meditate? What centers you?

Jeffrey Hayzlett: I work. When I'm in South Dakota I do a lot of outside work — that is a real workout! I haul, brush, cut trees, pull fence, move rocks—there is always something to do on our acreage there.

Chris Dessi: Who do you consult to make hard decisions in business and in life?

Jeffrey Hayzlett: For the most part I look in the mirror because the person staring back is the one that has to make the decision. But I also have partners, and I try to consult them.

Chris Dessi: I notice how hard you work, but I also notice that you love to spend time on your farm, and with your family. Now that you're a grandfather — How do you find a work/life balance? Have you always been able to separate church and state, or are you the type of guy that needs to schedule downtime — sort of force it upon yourself, so you don't burn out?

Jeffrey Hayzlett: Everything is about choices. I learned very early in life that you have to concentrate on living a balanced life. Stephen Covey once said, "a real successful leader balances between spiritual, friends, business, and family." I have a great partner, my wife of 33 years, who does a good job in keeping me centered and focused on the real things.

Chris Dessi: You've rubbed elbows with some of the most powerful people in the world (Donald Trump and Gene Simmons come to mind). Who has impressed you the most? What was it about that person that impressed you?

Jeffrey Hayzlett: To be very honest I don't get enamored much by the trappings of celebrities or high-powered people. In the end, they're just people. Maybe it's just a South Dakota thing; I treat everyone the same way I treat my next-door neighbor.

Chris Dessi: What's the biggest misconception young people have about success?

Jeffrey Hayzlett: I think it's being realistic about how hard you need to work. Most people don't succeed because they're lucky. They succeed because they're relentlessly hard workers. There is no real substitute for being great at what you do.

Chris Dessi: How important has your education been to your success? What do you say to people who say college is a waste of money?

Jeffrey Hayzlett: It's not a waste, it's an investment —if

you don't invest in yourself who else wants to invest in you? College helps lay the foundation for what you will do later in life, and your college or university friends will become lifelong friends.

Chris Dessi: What is one skill do you think all successful people MUST possess. Bar none.

Jeffrey Hayzlett: Listening.

SPEED ROUND

Chris Dessi: Dakota or New York?

Jeffrey Hayzlett: South Dakota

Chris Dessi: Donald Trump or Gene Simmons?

Jeffrey Hayzlett: While Gene is savvy and smart, Donald is relentless. Donald.

Chris Dessi: Bacon or …ah, never-mind.

Jeffrey Hayzlett: You had me at bacon.

Chris Dessi: Best compliment you ever received?

Jeffrey Hayzlett: Your children are wonderful.

Chris Dessi: In 100 years what one word do you think people will use to describe you?

Jeffrey Hayzlett: BIG!

Chris Dessi: What is your greatest strength or weakness?

Jeffrey Hayzlett: Focus, on both counts.

Chris Dessi: If you could travel back in time to witness anything — what would it be?

Jeffrey Hayzlett: Nothing—I want to live now, not then.

Chris Dessi: How do you break the ice at conferences when you meet new people?

Jeffrey Hayzlett: Hi, I am Jeffrey Hayzlett. I just walk up and say hello.

Chris Dessi: What's the strangest thing you've ever eaten?

Jeffrey Hayzlett: Taverns (Sloppy Joe's) my wife made. But they were made with love.

Chris Dessi: What's the longest you've ever gone without sleep?

Jeffrey Hayzlett: About four days. I don't want to do that again. Pre-Order Jeffrey's next book Think Big, Act Bigger now! Jeffrey Hayzlett is a primetime television host of C-Suite with Jeffrey Hayzlett and Executive Perspectives on C-Suite TV, and business radio host of All Business with Jeffrey Hayzlett on CBS on-demand radio network Play. It. He is a global business celebrity, speaker, best-selling author, and Chairman of C-Suite Network, home of the world's most powerful network of C-Suite leaders. Hayzlett is a well-traveled public speaker, the author of two bestselling business books, The Mirror Test and Running the Gauntlet. His third book, Think Big, Act Bigger, was released September 2015. Hayzlett is one of the most compelling figures in business today.

Uncommon Success Secrets From Dave Kerpen — An Entrepreneur in the Trenches

DAVE KERPEN

Founder & CEO, Likeable Local, NY Times Best-Selling Author & Speaker

My next "Success" interview is with Dave Kerpen. I admire Dave and all that he's accomplished. I first became aware of Dave and his agency during my tenure at Buddy Media. I had been able to get to know Dave via his prolific writing. However, Dave and I didn't meet in person until only a few months ago.

If you read any online business outlet, Dave is a regular contributor. Forbes, Inc.com, you name it — Dave has a loyal following. Silverback recently engaged Dave to keynote our Westchester Digital Summit. I knew he would be great. Our audience loved Dave. Dave also does a few things *differently* that intrigued me. In a world of super- ficial "liking" and "following" Dave *engages*. Upon first meeting him in the Likeable offices he drew me in. He's whip smart, and a powerhouse sales person. His wife is his business partner; he has high profile clients, and he had three kids at home. In our "always on" world that we live in, how does Dave do it all?

Excited to learn Dave's secrets to success, I went a little overboard with my questioning. Good thing I caught him while he was flying. He was gracious enough to spend the time to answer each inquiry. So who is this guy? What makes him tick? And does he really own 31 pairs of orange shoes? Let's find out. Here we go.

Chris Dessi: Dave, currently as I write this, your most popular post on Linkedin has over 2. 7million views. What is it about your writing that you feel resonates with the Linkedin community?

Dave Kerpen: I try to write simply and concisely, and I like to tell stories. If my kids can read a LinkedIn post of mine, that's a good thing.

Chris Dessi: You recently keynoted at my event, the West- chester Digital Summit. During your keynote, you discuss the importance of gratitude. What role does gratitude play in your everyday life?

Dave Kerpen: I'm a huge believer in gratitude. I hand write three thank-you cards each morning, and spend each dinner with my family going around the table, all sharing someone we're grateful for that day. Gratitude is the best drug on the planet.

Chris Dessi: You're a true family man, and you're business partners with your wife. What has that been like? How have you and your wife navigated the bumps in the road?

Dave Kerpen: It was very challenging at first — we brought arguments from home to work, and arguments from work to home. But with practice, we've become much better communicators and leaders. Ultimately, it's been amazing to share my businesses with my life partner.

Chris Dessi: You're what I call "Aggressively transparent" in your writing. Did this come naturally, or was this advice that someone shared? Why should my readers become more transparent in their blogging etc?

Dave Kerpen: Transparency is quite freeing, and a great differentiator. Most people are afraid to be radically transparent. So if you can open up and share your heart, people will respond to that.

Chris Dessi: You've been a successful entrepreneur for a few years now. You were once a school teacher. What facilitated that shift for you? Was there one defining moment, or was a gradual progression? Do you think you were a born entrepreneur?

Dave Kerpen: Our wedding was the biggest factor that took me from teacher to entrepreneur. I think I always had entrepreneurial tendencies, but after pulling off a sponsored wedding that raised $100,000 including $20,000 for charity, I knew we could build real businesses.

I'm still super passionate about education and hope to one-day support public schools as a public servant. Perhaps my next career.

Chris Dessi: You're a thought leader in digital and social

media. You contribute to Inc. om and even Forbes. How important has writing been to your success?

Dave Kerpen: Writing has been critical to my success. Writing has helped me to become a better thinker, which in turn has helped me to become a better leader. Writing bestselling books and well-read articles has also helped to position me as credible.

Chris Dessi: When was the first time you felt you were a success?

Dave Kerpen: I still don't feel like a success a lot of the time. There's always lots of room for improvement, you know? But the first time Likeable won "Best Places to Work" in New York from Crain's — that felt pretty awesome.

Chris Dessi: How do you define success?

Dave Kerpen: Success is being happy at the end of the day with what you've got!

Chris Dessi: I have two young daughters, as do you (now the Kerpens have welcomed a bouncing baby boy to their klan). How important do you think it is for young women to get involved as entrepreneurs? Is this something you discuss at home? Or does business never creep into your home life?

Dave Kerpen: We have "entrepreneurial" in our family mission statement, and it's one of our core values. My daughters are on their 3rd business right now. I've done several lessons on entrepreneurship with my 6th grader and 60 of her classmates, and my 2nd grader and 11 of her fellow girls scouts. So, I'd say it's pretty darn important to us as a family. I think that young women (and young men!) should be strongly encouraged to pursue entrepreneurship and that entrepreneurship, as creative problem solving, should be taught in every school in this country.

Chris Dessi: How great a role do you think luck has played in your success?

Dave Kerpen: I've been very lucky-most of all, to find Carrie to want to marry me and be my partner in all things. I married up at least two levels.

Chris Dessi: You're a successful guy — and a former school teacher, so you've taken academics seriously. What do you say to the pundits who feel that college is a waste of money?

Dave Kerpen: I think college is a waste of money, for many! I was fortunate enough to attend BU on a full scholarship. Otherwise, I could not have afforded it. I think that for many families, college provides an opportunity for structure and socialization and learning that works. I also think that got many, it's not necessary, or even beneficial. Personally, I would much rather spend $250,000 to fund a smart business plan that my future 18-year-old daughter is passionate about than fund four years of school for her. But we'll see about that!

Chris Dessi: Do you have brother and sisters? Where did you grow up? How has that shaped your successes?

Dave Kerpen: I grew up in Brooklyn, New York before it was cool, in Sunset Park with two younger brothers.

Dave & his brothers

My father has struggled a lot with bipolar disorder since

I was 12. So I learned at a very young age to be independent and to be a leader — I had to help take care of my younger brothers. I'm super impressed and proud of the young men they've become — Phil is a conservative leader in Washington and Dan is a technology marketer!

Chris Dessi: You seem to be living the American dream. What has that journey been like? Tell me about the lows — where there bumps along the way?

Dave Kerpen: There have been lots of lots of bumps along the way — and there still are bumps, every week! My wife Carrie talks about the "highlight reel" — you see people's highlights online and even in person, but you don't hear about the bumps as much. The first time I met Carrie, I fell madly in love with her, but she was married at the time. That sucked. When I went on 31 episodes of Paradise Hotel (Fox, 2003), I was famous for a bit, but when People Magazine called me "homely," that sucked. When I lost my first $500,000 client for going above her head, that sucked. When we nearly missed payroll, that sucked. Lots of bumps. But fortunately, lots of highs too!

Chris Dessi: Are there people in your life who inspire your success? Tell me about them.

Dave Kerpen: I'm inspired by great leaders — Mark Zuckerberg, Tony Hsieh, and Jeff Weiner, to name a few. As for people I know more intimately, my wife Carrie is my greatest inspiration. I've also been blessed to be surrounded by great mentors and advisors. My father in law, the late Honorable Steven Fisher, taught me to show your friendship first, and the late Senator Frank

Lautenberg taught me that family is our greatest legacy.

Chris Dessi: What's your rythm? What time do you go to bed? Do you meditate? If not — when and how do you find quiet time? When do you wake up? Do you exercise? If so — what do you do to keep fit & stay focused?

Dave Kerpen: I don't sleep much. I typically go to sleep at 1 am or so and wake up at 6. I've struggled to embrace meditation, and I never have quiet time. I hate to relax. That's probably why I need to meditate. I need to exercise more! I love to play tennis, but get bored by most other forms of exercise.

Chris Dessi: Your writing offers so much great insight for entrepreneurs. I hear from many whose businesses are failing. They're about to give up. Can you share a moment when you were about to give up? What kept you going? What would you give to these entrepreneurs as advice to keep going?

Dave Kerpen: I have moments where I want to give up all the time. I try to embrace those moments instead of avoiding them. For example, a month ago, an investor who I was sure was going to invest $1 million in our new business Likeable Local, pulled out at the last minute. That sucked a lot, be made me want to give up. But our mission to help small businesses inspires me, as do the amazing people I'm proud to call my team. So there's just no giving up! To entrepreneurs who feel like giving up, I say, the number one most important trait that defines whether you're successful or not is persistence. You can do it.

Chris Dessi: You public speak often. You seem like a natural. Are you? Or have you had to work at it. If so, what advice can you offer those who want to be better public speakers?

Dave Kerpen: I love to speak — the bigger the crowd, the bigger the high I get. That said, like anything, practice has made me better. I've had a speaking coach who helped me to realize, that it's never about me, and always about the audience.

Chris Dessi: You're a prolific content creator — books, blogs, articles, etc. When do you find the time? What's your writing schedule look like? Are you an everyday no matter what type of blogger? Or are you able to put in great effort around deadlines.

Dave Kerpen: I write late at night typically (11pm-1am) or early in the morning (5am-8am), and on planes. I'm writing this long interview response on a plane.

Chris Dessi: You're super laid back and easy to get along with. One may say that you're "Likeble." How important do you think it is for today's leaders to be likeable?

Dave Kerpen: In an increasingly transparent and fast-changing world, it's essential for leaders to be like-able. I feel so strongly about this, I wrote a book about it, Like-able Business.

Chris Dessi: Would you go back to teaching?

Dave Kerpen: Yes, I

would love to teach again. Or start a school and be a principal. Or be a superintendent of schools somewhere. Or be the Secretary of Education.

Chris Dessi: Why orange?

Dave Kerpen: Orange is the most positive persuasive color. Plus, my 31 pairs of orange shoes help me stand out a bit.

SPEED ROUND

Q. Yankees or Mets?
A. METS!

Q. What's the best advice you've ever received?
A. Show your friendship first.

Q. Do you have a life motto?
A. Just be likeable.

Q. What cheers you up?
A. My kids, and feeling grateful.

Q. Favorite word?
A. Likeable. (duh)

Q. What are the names of your children, and what significance do those names have to you and your wife?
A. Charlotte is my oldest though technically she's my step-daughter since her birth father is my wife's ex-husband. She was named after her great aunt. Kate was

named after my grandpa, and Seth Franklin, my one-month-old, was named after my two mentors above, my father in law Steven Fisher and Senator Frank Lautenberg.

Q. What's your worst vice?
A. Gambling.

Q. Good book, or Netflix?
A. House of Cards.

Q. Game of Thrones or Breaking Bad?
A. Orange is the New Black.

Q. EQ or IQ?
A. EQ

Pitch Anything Author Oren Klaff on Success

OREN KLAFF

Author of Pitch Anything, Managing Director at
Intersection Capital

I'm an avid reader. Actually, I'm lying. I'm an avid audio-book listener. I'm a full blown Audible.com maniac. I consume anywhere from 25-35 books a year while I'm driving to and from the office. I love spending my driving time this way. I feel productive, and I get amazing ideas for my business. I feel as if I earn a master's degree every six months thanks to my dedication to educational audio files. The habit keeps me sharp. I've credited some of my books to saving my sanity and at times saving my business. About a year ago I listened to Oren Klaff's book Pitch Anything. Afterward, I did something that I don't do. *I listened to it again.* Then I listened to it again. I passed it on to my CMO. I recommended it to anyone who would listen. I wrote a blog post about it. Finally, I began implementing its principles. My business began growing beyond anything I could have imagined. Recently, I connected with Oren Klaff on Twitter. Last week — Oren chatted with me about success. We even discussed writing a book together. During our chat — we covered everything from Millennials to the Matrix. Please keep your hands and feet inside the vehicle at all times. Buckle up, and come along for a ride. . . on the Oren side. Please welcome Oren Klaff.

Chris Dessi: In your biography it states you raised close to half a billion dollars. You don't need the money. Why write the book Pitch Anything?

Oren Klaff: For fame and fortune! The time I wrote the book (2009 early 2010) — the deal business was dead. There was nothing to do but watch time go by, and then somebody saw me speak. They said — you should do a radio show with Howard Stern. I didn't like radio because you're talking to jobless losers at 3 pm in the afternoon. Then someone said — how about do a book? What else is there to do when there is nothing going on? It's been fun.

Chris Dessi: The tactics that your teaching and using they can be pretty intense. Are you concerned that some people will crash and burn if they're mishandling the techniques your teaching?

Oren Klaff: Have you watched the show Pros vs. Joes? You have these weekend athletes, ridiculously in shape, like 2% body fat, ex-marines. They put them on a playing field with ex-pro-athletes. You get to see the difference between the guy that's just super in shape and a pro. The thing is — the pros completely manhandled these guys.completely overwhelming them. If you look at the best amateur athlete out of context, you think, *"hey this guys looks like he could play pro ball."* Then you look in context with a pro player, and he looks silly, those guys just destroy them.

Nothin in the book works without first getting the experience of pushing on people a little bit and creating a some tension. You have to take it easy, though. There are a lot of things to do before you can get aggressive with people. So, yes, I do see people taking it out of context, but for the most part, people take it seriously, they don't get over their skies. We get dozens of emails a day saying, *"the book changed my life. I took it slow, I implemented the stuff, now I'm I'm a monster, and I'm killing. Nobody stands in my way, and I have you to thank for it."*

Chris Dessi: Right — they skip steps. In the book, you touch on it but you don't go to those steps. Is that why you have the webinars? Or is there a follow-up book in the works — with tactical steps?

Oren Klaff: No, no. So here's the thing: the book is my vision. It's like that scene in The Matrix with the key maker — you open one door, and it's an ice landscape. Close it and open it again, and it's like a summer spring mountain Germany castle view. Close it and open it again, and it's an interstellar night sky. The job of the book is to let you know that there's a matrix out there. That the world as you know it is not fixed and full of boundaries in the way that you think it is. You can say things and do things, and there are ways to change people's behaviors that you never thought was were possible.

Before, you could say, (meekly) *"Hey, thank you so much for having me here at your business; I'm so excited to present you our material today. I hope you choose us as your vendor, and if you do I'll work extra hard and the customers are always right and we'll bend over backward to make you happy. Here's my pager number, here's my cell phone, here's my fax machine. I'll always be available all week and just choose us and we will do whatever it takes to make you happy."*

That's sort of how people believe you should behave in front to of a buyer. So, if you open this door to the matrix and believe that, (confidently) *"Hey guys, can you get the boss in here cause it's time to roll. I'm super busy, and I have to get somewhere else in an hour from now. We have a lot to cover; grab your guys, I have my guys, lets roll. I got an agenda. Let's go through it,"* is the only thing you can say.

Chris Dessi: Cool. So you mentioned something that I liked. That the book may be more about self-mastery. What is your personal rhythm? Do you meditate? Do you visualize?

Oren Klaff: Yeah, really good question. You do not want to take my path at being great. I had to use trial and error and lose a lot of deals and do a lot of suffering because I didn't know what was possible. I had to try to get to what was possible. So it took many many years, it was slow. The reality is, I was a computer programmer. Both my parents are academics. My dad is a statistician. He is not a boxer. I did not play on the high school football team. Girls didn't like me in high school. I didn't drive a Camaro. I was a nerd. Over time, I realized that's not a good state to be in. Where your supplicating, having to ask people for things, having them say no and you're going "ok." That's horrible. So slowly, I got on the path of improving and it was far too slow.

The job of Pitch Anything is to accelerate that. But I started out where everybody else starts — in suckville. And Chris I see a lot of people say I'm gonna get out of loserville population "me" through manipulation. I talked to a guy yesterday. They have a pretty good sales organization. They ran me through their pitch. Everything is so Robert Cialdini. It's so clearly manipulative. I mean the great thing about pitching is that it's fun! That is my motivation. I am always having fun! Around me is a hemisphere of fun. If you step into my hemisphere, say, within 20 feet of me and I stop having fun. You need to get the fuck out. Okay? That's my rule; I'm having fun!

Chris Dessi: When you're having fun have you ever had somebody get offended?

Oren Klaff: If you have that rule you have to accept lies. This is the problem with salespeople. Because they can't accept that it may not be a good fit. You have to say it's just not a good account. I don't want it. Yes, I'd make my numbers, yes, I'd make my commission, yes, I'd be able to buy the car I want to get or whatever. But It's not a good account. I'm not going to have fun! They don't want me to make margin, they're not going to be easy to work with, and there are better ways to live.

Now you're free; you don't give a fuck.

You say, (confidently) *"There's nobody that knows more about ball bearings and spinning Kevlar and metallurgy and tractor-trailer parts and how to ship pack and install them. Nobody knows that stuff better than me and really like it or hate it. I'm in demand people want my time because I'm the best at this. So I have to be picky in who I work with."*

Chris Dessi: So it's about the ability to have a tolerance

that you may lose the deal. Because if they're offended — then they just weren't the right people to be working with. Is that true?

Oren Klaff: Yeah, that's right. If they get offended, it means they don't have the money. Now, we're in a sophisticated step; this is the moral authority print. When you paint yourself right down the middle, and you paint the other guy as unusual, then two things can happen.

> • They were never a buyer in the first place; they're just pricing you out.
> • They try to come back to the center where you are.

Nobody wants to be painted as weird cute unusual and outside the norm in their behavior. So yea these are the controls for sure. I was listening to a song during CrossFit. The lyrics are, *"I don't give a fuck because I'm dangerous, I don't have any more cocaine to take so I'm dangerous. I ran out of beer, so I'm dangerous. I don't have a car, so I'm a guys who don't care are free and dangerous."*

That's you if you don't care. If you believe the buyer has control over you and can make you happy by awarding you a contract, then you are in a vulnerable position. Now, I'm not saying walk in and don't give a fuck. I'm saying walk in and care. Care about the right things. Care about the fact that you are happy, that you're having fun! That you're allowed to give the buyer a good product, make a margin and have him be successful with it. That the relationship works for both sides. That's what you care about, that's centrist, that's right in the middle, that's plain manila envelope what everybody wants, and that is what's fair. If the buyer wants something that's not fair, then you should start to back away.

- The greater pitch creates a big funnel.
- A big funnel reduces your neediness.
- The reduction of neediness makes it more likely that the buyer will come in on your terms.

If you read the book, I lay out for you in very clear simple terms how you can get it and start using it.

Chris Dessi: Two minutes left and I want to get to how do you define success. But before that you mentioned Cross-Fit. Do you exercise? If so what do you do to keep fit?

Oren Klaff: I work out at the navy seal training center Seal Fit here in southern California. It's a very rigorous program that keeps you pretty busy. I'm not going to get into life balance, but if you don't have life balance it's very difficult to feel like you've got control of the center. I have 20 motorcycles, and I have cars … the truth is, once you get it, it's nice but you don't need it. What you need, (and this is my definition of success), is to do your work, step away, look back on it, be proud of it, and then go get your other stuff.

The reason you need those things is because you have a center. And it's okay to get off center. It's okay to go off on warped benders. It's okay to get beside yourself and test new territories. But if you don't know where your center is you don't know where to come back to. If you look at these celebrities that have done plastic surgery — like Lindsay Lohan. Because as much as you want to love her she, doesn't have a center to come back to. She's doing plastic surgery, or she's doing behavior and that's her new center, but the next one doesn't seem that far off. And that's where people you know get way off.

Why isn't that person looking in a mirror? Yeah, they have a mirror, they just don't have a center.

Your center is:

- Something you like doing
- Something you have passion about
- Someone you love

You can always come to that and calibrate yourself. Hopefully, that was helpful. I know for some millennials they say "I wanna make money. I want a Ferrari. I want a house on Manhattan Beach. I want a jet." Those are good ideals. I respect the consumerism and the wanting to make money, but at some point I also have to have a center because I'll just add — most of that stuff is luck.

A Storied Career of Global Success

BILL LAROSA
CEO/Executive Leadership Coach, Business/Personal
Growth Consultant, Experienced Public Board Director
& Angel Investor

When I was five, my Uncle would chase me around his house, rough housing with my brother and I. He drove us around in his red MG. He had vanity plates that read "Bill's MG."

I thought he was super cool.

When I was ten, my Uncle pulled out a shoebox. An unimaginable pile of old passports spilled out. I began sifting through them. Stamps from Rome, Paris, London, Japan, China, Australia, etc, etc, etc. He'd been to countries I didn't even know existed. Places I hadn't heard of before. He'd been to each *two times over*.

I was in awe.

When I was 20, I was living and studying in Leuven, Belgium. I wanted to see the world just like my Uncle. He took me out for dinner in Brussels. We ordered Duck, drank Belgian beer, and chatted up pretty women.

I wanted to be him.

When I was 30 my Uncle and I spent an afternoon on a golf course in Austin, Texas. I grilled him. What was it like when you were in Brazil? What year did you visit Africa for the first time? What did you learn while in the executive program at GE in the 60's?

I wanted to learn everything from him.

At 40, I got to ask him every burning question I had built up about his career. His big wins, some losses, and everything between. He's had a storied business career that has taken him around the world. He broke free from humble beginnings in Brooklyn, NY. No Ivy League education. No monied pedigree. Just a definitive chip on his Italian-American shoulder and a will to scrap, scrape and scratch his way to the top.

G. William LaRosa is not just my Uncle. He's my Godfather. I've idolized him for as long as I can remember.

Recently, in the midst of a compelling conversation about business, I marveled at his intellect. He replied,

"I'm not that smart, I've just been around."

I call that *wisdom*.

It's my honor to share my Godfather's wisdom with you.

Chris Dessi: You grew up in Brooklyn. I asked another Brooklyn native Rosanna Scotto — what is it with our national obsession over Brooklyn? Can you put into words why people are so fascinated with the borough?

Bill LaRosa: Brooklyn is a state of mind. It was the foundation of all I was to become or might have been. It is now a memory of my foundation as much as it is an aspiration. For me, the memory was a cross between West Side Story, the Goodfellas and Happy Days. I have often returned to Brooklyn — especially when things were not going so well in my life — to walk the streets where I was raised and played to ground myself. It helped a lot to walk those streets. I could hear my friends calling, and smell the  Italian cooking spewing from the open, summer, windows (before air-conditioning).

Chris Dessi: You've been a senior executive in corporate America, an entrepreneur, and an advisor. In the process, you've been able to travel the world. Was traveling always your goal, or did travel just manifest because of your profession? Tell us about that journey.

Bill LaRosa: Traveling at first was an adventure, the thrill of going somewhere I'd never been before. At that time, it was all about the destination. There were so many private moments where I stared into an airplane or hotel bathroom mirror and wondered what the heck a kid from Brooklyn was doing in Zaire, Rio, Paris, Singapore, Sydney and so many more places I had only dreamed about. After awhile when the airline million mile awards started to appear the trips remained exciting because even though I had been to most places numerous times it was now about the excitement of dealing with so many different cultures. Today I've planted my roots in Austin. I purposely don't travel much anymore. I've had enough. Now I watch my friends take their dream trips to Paris and Rome and realize how fortunate I've been.

Chris Dessi: I speak with many successful executives that question the value of college. You have an undergraduate degree from Manhattan College as well as an MBA from Pace University. What do you say to those detractors of education?

Bill LaRosa: I believe one must follow their passions. Sometimes those passions don't include college That's ok, but when folks don't know their passion it's a good insurance policy to get an education. Maybe en route a passion or two will evolve. But if you are among those who don't yet know your passion, at least get a degree that is practical and you can make a living from it. If that evades you as well, go to a trade school and learn a trade. I know millionaires who are plumbers, construction workers, restaurant owners, and electricians.

Chris Dessi: How do you define success?

Bill LaRosa: Doing what you love to do every day surrounded by people who love you and whom you love in return.

Chris Dessi: Can you explain the impact, if any, that social networking has made on your career and you personally.

Bill LaRosa: Frankly I don't think it has made a lot of difference in my business career. It's a source of fun so far in my personal life with Facebook pictures and all. I have connected with many friends from my early childhood on Facebook. As far as business is concerned,  I'm y getting a face lift on my website. So come back to me in a year and I'll let you know what return I get on that.

Chris Dessi: How much of your success was due to luck? Or are you of the mindset that you create your luck?

Bill LaRosa: I never had a career plan per se. I developed two traits early in life, which I suspect helped me along the way. The first was persistence. I was never the smartest or the most gifted person in the room but, recognizing that, I was determined to work the hardest to at least be considered as a candidate for those positions I targeted on the playing field or corpo-  rate America. The 2nd was flexibility. I was always flexible. And I was blessed with a wife and family who supported me and allowed me to follow those opportunities that in turn provided them a not-so-bad lifestyle.

Chris Dessi: Did you have a mentor when you first started out? How important do you think mentorship is for all executives?

Bill LaRosa: I didn't have a mentor in the traditional sense ever. I wish I did. Over the years, I worked for some terrific people and some not so terrific ones also. I learned a lot from the good guys and even more from the bad ones. I consider myself a life-long learner and a student of everything that peaks my interest at any given time. I am a little OCD and delve deep into stuff I like. Ok, I'm more than a little OCD.

Chris Dessi: When did you first think of yourself as a success?

Bill LaRosa: Tomorrow

Chris Dessi: Many young executive struggle with work life/balance — myself included. What advice do you give them? How did you strike a balance?

Bill LaRosa: Find yourself a life partner and soul mate that supports you and then you work like hell to make sure you and your family are taken care of. It's best if those two are the same person. The only balance there is to all that, is to make sure you don't lose your family as you provide the best for them. How do you do that? Each one of us is different, and there is no formula..... figure it out, you're on your own, but it's one of the most important things you will figure out.

Chris Dessi: On paper your resume reads like success, after success. Can you tell us about your biggest failure? How did it change you or shift your approach moving forward?

Bill LaRosa: I suppose I've had my share of "failures" but I guess I never looked at them that way. I've made tons of mistakes and have had bad things happen to me. But I've never considered them failure per se. The mistakes I've owned and tried to learn from, and the bad things, well, one tries to understand why things happened and although it's harder, try to learn something from those as well. But learning is not where it stops, in order to benefit from these things. I've learned to change my behavior in order to cause real change. That's the tough part. And the older you get, the tougher that becomes.

Chris Dessi: Who has been the greatest positive influence on your life? Tell us about that person.

Bill LaRosa: My father. Wow. Where do i begin?

Chris Dessi: You're an avid reader. Always pushing yourself to learn more via books/audiobooks. How do you find the time, and what advice can you offer my readers who think they don't have time to improve themselves with reading.

Bill LaRosa: No one has the time. One makes the time. If you don't take that time to read to learn you never sharpen your ax and eventually you and it becomes so dull you find you cannot achieve much anymore. If you don't take the time to read to enjoy or relax, you can never re-energize your batteries.

Chris Dessi: What do you think is the one characteristic that all the successful people you know share?

Bill LaRosa: Persistence

Chris Dessi: You have 20 minutes to sit alone in a room with the 21-year-old Bill LaRosa. He's just graduated from college, and he's about to embark on a career that will take him around the world. What advice do you give him?

Bill LaRosa: Keep a journal, take lots of pictures and keep them in a safe place, never quit, enjoy the ride and buy lots of Austin real estate in zip code 78704

Chris Dessi: For someone who has seen great monetary success — what do you think is dangerous about that type of success?

Bill LaRosa: At some point there's enough but for many the feeling is there's never enough. The danger lies in the latter feeling. The reality and peace lie in the former.

Chris Dessi: How important are habits and routine to your success father? What is your Rhythm? What time do you go to bed? Do you exercise? Do you meditate?

Bill LaRosa: I do Bikram (i. e., Hot) Yoga. I call it the boot camp of yoga. It has changed my chemistry for the better, my body for the better and my mind. I sleep 7-8 hrs. Per night, and try to meditate whenever I can.

Chris Dessi: How has your childhood (the way you were raised, your birth order) affected your career success? Did it at all?

Bill LaRosa: Yes, it's taught me persistence, focus, responsibility, loyalty to family, country and God, especially family.

Chris Dessi: As an Italian-American — have you ever had to overcome discrimination?

Bill LaRosa: One time years ago when trying to buy a house in Darien Connecticut. The realtor said to my wife and I she didn't have anything in this town to show us. That was almost verbatim even though she knew we had more than enough money to buy anything we wanted. I laugh at that moment now and wonder where she is today. With a perspective like that her lack of success in career and life was virtually assured.

Chris Dessi: You're an active Board Member, advisor, and investor in many companies. What advice do you give to young entrepreneurs who are looking to get funded?

Bill LaRosa: Develop something unique that you are passionate about. If it's unique and you believe people will pay for the benefits of what you will deliver, be persistent and tenacious in seeking every form of funding to launch and grow. An investor loves seeing money invested from the entrepreneur. From friends and family, from crowd funding, from any partners/employees etc.

Chris Dessi: What has been your greatest career success to date?

Bill LaRosa: My family.

Chris Dessi: Tell us about a time while traveling when you felt scared for your life? If ever.

Bill LaRosa: There were many times — Jeddah and Zaire in the late 70s were the worst. Some of the barrios in Rio during the same time come in a close second. Walking my date back home in Brooklyn, Bedford-Stuyvesant section in the 60 s regularly made me bead my rosary all the way to the subway station.

Chris Dessi: You've managed many people throughout your career. What advice would you give someone going into a leadership position for the first time?

Bill LaRosa: Be gen-
uine. Don't try to
be someone you're
not. Clearly under-
stand your objective
and desired results.
Listen to your
team's views on how
to achieve them.
Solicit the opinions

of others on the same. Decide on the alternatives, select
one, communicate it clearly to your team, assign KPIs to
each team member explaining how achieving them help
the overall mission, lead by example.

RAPID FIRE

Chris Dessi: I believe you have so much advice and guidance to offer for business people — will you ever write
your memoirs?

Bill LaRosa: Probably not, they'd be X-rated.

Chris Dessi: My daughters know that I hate witches —
what's one thing that scares the hell out of you?

Bill LaRosa: Heights. I skydived to try to overcome the
fear, but after 38 jumps I'm still scared to look over my
home office's 2nd-floor balcony

Chris Dessi: Best day of your life.

Bill LaRosa: Tomorrow

Chris Dessi: Worst day of your life?

Bill LaRosa: The day my father died. My dad died on my birthday. I made a horrible decision to prioritize a business's meeting in Geneva where I was living at the time over returning home at my family's request. Worst decision I ever made. I don't celebrate my birthday anymore. Instead I reflect upon my dad and the regrets of a very bad day

Chris Dessi: You have access to a time machine, but you can never come back to present day. You can go into the future, or into the past. Where do you go in time?

Bill LaRosa: Always the future. The future is a mystery; an adventure into your mind's perspective of things to come. I have always been more about the next adventure than the past

Chris Dessi: Favorite alcoholic beverage?

Bill LaRosa: Jack Daniels when I'm drinking, Bombay Safire Extra dry martini when I'm "dining" out (shaken, not stirred) and a light beer over ice with two lime wedges when the Texas heat says it time for an adult refreshment

Chris Dessi: You've lived both places — so I have to ask: Brooklyn or Austin?

Bill LaRosa: Austin. Brooklyn is the ME I was. Austin is the ME I commit to become

Chris Dessi: Name someone who knows more about you than anyone else in the world.

Bill LaRosa: My wife

Chris Dessi: Most powerful business book you've ever read that you recommend to everyone.

Bill LaRosa: Napoleon Hill: Think and grow rich. It says it all.

Chris Dessi: Country with the best-looking women (I had to ask).

Bill LaRosa: Sweden by a long shot. (Tall fit blondes… paradise)

Chris Dessi: Which is the most livable city (outside of the US)

Bill LaRosa: Geneva Switzerland

Chris Dessi: Best city to be an entrepreneur?

Bill LaRosa: San Jose California or Austin Texas (boom town, 800 people per day are coming here from all around)

Chris Dessi: Worst city you ever visited?

Bill LaRosa: Lagos

Chris Dessi: You've owned both — so I have to ask:

Bill LaRosa: Harley or Maserati? Harley … It's the closest feeling to flying on land

Success Lessons from a Television Executive Who's Seen it All

LEW LEONE
VP and General Manager at WNYW/WWOR-TV

Sometimes I get to go on TV. It's always a fun experi-ence. I get to meet interesting people. Some of those people are on set, while others are behind the scenes. Over the years, I've gotten to know Lew Leone, VP and General Manager at WNYW/WWOR-TV. He's engaging, intelligent, and wildly successful in the news business. He's also a nice Italian kid from New York — so, of course, we bonded immediately. Over the years, I would encoun-ter Lew in the hallway, and he would dive right into the topic at hand. Always with an opinion, a question, and an open mind. Lew impresses me. He has an Ivy League education — a great family — and a career he loves. In my mind, this is success.

I bring you Lew Leone — welcome.

Chris Dessi: As I write this, your title is VP & General Manager at WNYW/WWOR-TV. That's impressive. But of course, you didn't start off at the top. What has your journey been like? The highs, the lows, how did you end up here?

Lew Leone: I've had an incredible journey so far and consider myself extremely lucky. After college, I didn't really know what I wanted to do. My dad's friend Bob Calandruccio ran the buying arm of what was the essentially the first media buying service Vitt Media. He hired me as an assistant buyer, and I quickly learned the ins and outs of local TV and radio buying. It became clear to me that I belonged on the sell side of the business. I looked at some of the TV Station rep firms, but most of them required relocation, so I found a job at Avery-Knodel in NYC representing small NBC Affiliates and some sign-on independent stations. It was straight commission, and it was awesome. That led to a sales job at WABC-TV in 1985. I was by far the youngest person, and they called me "the kid" I thought I would stay at ABC for my entire career. I entered the "system" which was essentially a rotation to different jobs around the country. Chicago for three years and then St. Louis when we were acquired by Capital Cities. Cap Cities had a different philosophy regarding moves, and I was essentially stuck in St. Louis. I was going to leave and accept a job in NYC when I finally reached (there was no email then) Bill Cella, who was running ABC Sports Sales. I flew in a few days later, and he offered me a job. It was the heyday of ABC Sports. Monday Night Football, College Football, Triple Crown,

Indy 500, USGA Golf Package, Wide World of Sports. I had clients like Anheuser Busch, Nike, Microsoft and Burger King and negotiated huge deals. It was a dream job. In 1996, we were acquired by Disney. They fired Dennis Swanson, who was the President of ABC Sports, and then disaster struck. The Executive Producer of ABC Sports Jack O'Hara, his wife Janet and daughter 13-year-old Caitlin died aboard TWA Flight 800 on their way to The Tour de France, which was to be Jack's last assignment at ABC. Jack was not only a co-worker but a friend and high school football teammate. It was a very strange time for me. At that point, Dennis Swanson recruited me to join him at WNBC-TV as a local sales manager. My boss was Frank Comerford one of the greatest salesmen of all time. After that, I did an 18-month stint in the number two role at NBC Network Sports Sales as VP, Sports and Olympic Sales. When Frank Comerford got promoted, I returned to WNBC as VP Sales. At WNBC, we set a record for single station TV revenue and margin which will never be repeated. We had a 71% margin in 1999 and then the dot-com bubble burst. In 2002, Dennis Swanson and I exited NBC on the same day he became COO of the CBS Station Group, and I became President, WCBS-TV. It was my first GM job, and I felt extremely well prepared as we initiated a major turnaround at WCBS. Three years later I was presented with an opportunity to work for Jack Abernethy running Fox's New York Duopoly of WNYW and WWOR-TV. I jumped at the chance. I've been with Fox for almost ten years, and I love what I do and who I work for.

Chris Dessi: Is this always what you wanted to do? If so, who did you want to emulate? Did you have a mentor?

Lew Leone: When I started at WABC-TV in 1985 I thought it would be pretty cool to be the GM of a New York City TV Station but since by definition there are only a handful of those jobs I knew it would be a longshot. Throughout my career, I've had many different opportunities but somehow I kept getting pulled back to local television. Dennis Swanson was clearly one of the all-time great TV Station General Managers. He is the guy who put WLS-TV the ABC owned station in Chicago on the map by launching Oprah Winfrey's career and playing Jeopardy and Wheel of Fortune in the prime access time period. He followed that up by taking WNBC to the number one position in New York. Dennis is well known for his integrity, work ethic, tenacity and desire to win. He values loyalty and family. He has been a great mentor to me.

Chris Dessi: What do you think will be the most enduring thing you've done? What I mean is: in 100 Years from now we look back on your career, what do you hope your legacy will be?

Lew Leone: I think I've been able to connect with the community through interaction with many diverse groups. I feel that I always try to help whoever asks. Certainly since they are on video, I hope my editorials will prove that I knew what I was talking about.

Chris Dessi: How important has your family (wife/kids) been to your success? Do you bring your work home, or have you been able to create a clear work/life balance?

Lew Leone: We had very young children when I worked for ABC Sports, and that job required a good dose of weekend travel to sporting events. It was tough on my wife in those days because I was off having a great time and she took on all of the child rearing. By definition as a TV Station GM you are on call 24/7. When the phone rings at 2 am, it is never good news. However, I've been able to do things like coach my kids and recently I served on my local school board, so it has been doable.

Chris Dessi: You're active in your community (Scarsdale), how important is it for young families to get involved in the politics/policy of their local school district?

Lew Leone: Most people don't pay attention until they have kids in school. In New York City, it is very difficult to affect change but it is different in School Districts where citizens get a chance to vote on their School Budget and for their Board Trustees. I would urge young families to get involved, attend a few meetings, join the PTA and get to know the faculty and staff in your district.

Chris Dessi: You host a popular segment on Fox 5 called Lew's view. You state that your views aren't necessary those of the station. What do you say to detractors who say that this is a conflict of interest and that you should report the news, not comment on it?

Lew Leone: Every newspaper has an editorial column. That's akin to what I do with Lew's Views. I'm not a journalist just a regular guy. I think Viewers appreciate that I have a point of view. It also gives a name to the guy behind the scenes. I guess if people think I'm a jerk then they will not watch but I respect everyone's opinion, and I answer questions and connect with our audience.

Chris Dessi: How are you and your staff working to stay relevant in a medium that for young people has become secondary, or even worse — completely obsolete? How has technology (social media) changed programming during your tenure? How are you working to stay relevant?

Lew Leone: Young people have never really embraced Television News so what you had were young viewers of traditional TV who grew up and turned to news when they got married, had kids and paid taxes. Now you have young people who have never watched traditional TV but who will care about our content when they get older. We have to be readily available with our content on every platform. Our advantage is that we produce 8 hours of live local content every day. Our challenge is to make sure that our content is relevant and serves the needs of a mobile audience who want to know what is going on from a credible source.

Chris Dessi: I find you to be highly intelligent, but more importantly very personable, engaging and relatable. Genuinely fun to chat/banter with. Do you work at this? I guess what I'm asking is — are you a "How to Win Friends and Influence People" type of guy, or do you think it just comes naturally to you? If this doesn't come naturally to some, what advice can you give them?

Lew Leone: Both of my parents are super sales people. My mom in Real Estate and my dad Life Insurance. My dad used to eat dinner with us as a family and then go out and sell insurance in people's living rooms. I was at an event recently, and I introduced myself (my dad is Lew Sr.) and the guy said "Lew Leone? Let me tell you about Lew Leone. On the day I got home from my honeymoon, your dad knocked on my door and sold me an insurance policy and I ended up buying three more from him. It was the best thing I ever did. Now I get a nice check every month" They taught me the art of engaging with and talking to just about anyone. I've also learned from some of the best sales people in the business. I continue to learn especially as it relates to making connections in the world of social media. For young people, I can't stress enough the value of connecting in person, asking questions and genuinely listening. In fact, I just read a nice post from Gary Vaynerchuck on Networking.

Chris Dessi: As I write this you have 2,438 followers on a very active Twitter account. How important has social media been for you? Do you think every newsperson should be on social media?

Lew Leone: I jumped in late to social media, but I used Lew's Views as a way to engage. It has proven to be a very valuable tool to connect with viewers, influencers and causes and I continue to find ways for my interactions to add value to my day job and my life. For instance a women I have never met @sallypancakes told me on Twitter that I should just show up at a November Project workout. It is a free fitness movement for people of all abilities, and it will change your life. Still waiting for Julia La Roche aka Sally Pancakes to show up. Every newsperson must use social media.

Chris Dessi: You have degree from Princeton University — arguably one of the finest universities in the world. What do you say to those who feel that college is a waste of time? How much of your success do you attribute to your time at Princeton?

Lew Leone: I once received an award from Bill Cella the then-President of ABC Sports Sales. It was a plaque of me throwing my Princeton Diploma in the trash. I was a great High School athlete who

used that to get into college. I had never been west of Pennsylvania and had one trip on an airplane to Dartmouth in March of my senior year. For me, the value of College was exposure to a huge diversity of incredibly smart people. I was blown away by how smart people were. I think you can argue that College is too expensive, but it is certainly not a waste of time.

Chris Dessi: Tomorrow you wake up, and you're Mayor. What are the top three priorities your administration focuses on to ensure New York's success?

Lew Leone: As Mayor of New York City my priorities would be Education-It is disgraceful that we are failing so many kids. Quality of Living — I want NYer's to be safe and proud of their city and lastly I would work to make NYC a more business-friendly environment and that includes improvements in public transportation.

Chris Dessi: Guy walks into your office for an interview — top of his class at Princeton. He's a genius, best guy for the job and will surely get you promoted. You will make you lots of money from this hire— but he shows up for the interview in shorts, flip flops and tank top. Do you give him the job?

Lew Leone: Does he have any tattoos? Look. A few years ago it would be a hard no. I like to think that I'm evolving with the times and have more of an open mind.

Chris Dessi: What's your daily rhythm? What time are you in bed, what time do you wake up? Do you exercise? Meditate? How do you stay on top of it all?

Lew Leone: During the week I'm usually in bed by 10:30. Usual wake up is 5 am unless I'm closing in on a race then I move it up 4:30 am. Drive to NYC for a workout which is swim, bike, run or November Project and then in the office around 8 or 8:15. I would like to meditate more often, but I use the same lame excuse that I can't find 10 minutes. I like to be busy. If I'm not busy then I lose track of things. Does that make sense?

Chris Dessi: How do you define Success?

Lew Leone: I define success by being able to look in the mirror and know that you have done the best you can.

Chris Dessi: Working in news is a difficult task. Have you ever thought "enough it enough" . . I'm outta here? Or do you think it's in your blood — either you're in it or you're dead?

Lew Leone: I just watch the news and our competition. The real warriors are the photographers and reporters who are in the field gathering the news. Being on scene at some of the tougher stories can get to you but, for the most part, that's where the true news hounds want to be.

Chris Dessi: What has been you shining moment in news? What are you most proud of? I guess I'm asking — what has been your greatest success/achievement? Publically and personally? Is it the same? Why?

Lew Leone: I'm most proud of the fact that our little local show Good Day New York was able to beat the behemoths Good Morning America and The Today Show. Yes, it is the same. Personally I took satisfaction because I hired the people that did it.

Chris Dessi: You've met heads of state, and major movie stars. Who has been the most fascinating person you've encountered, and why?

Lew Leone: I think it has to be Wendy Williams. To go

from drug addict to major star and business mogul is a truly fascinating story. I used to laugh very hard with her on the radio and was amazed at how smart she was. And now to witness her work ethic, drive, and determination to succeed, in person, has been an inspiration. I always tell people that Wendy is the real deal.

Chris Dessi: News is a tough business. What do you say to young college graduates looking to break into news? Where should they start? How can they impress you, and get your attention? What does that skill set look like?

Lew Leone: News is a tough business. Technology has turned everyone into video news gatherers, editors, producers, writers, and reporters and that's just with an iPhone. Often time's young people have all of these skills but we have multiple people doing them. We need to adapt faster and become more efficient. Right now the most valuable people in a news organization are report-ers with contacts who get the story right. My advice is to listen to Chris Dessi and start a blog.

Chris Dessi: They decide they're going to make a movie of your life story. Which actor would you choose to play young Lew Leone — present day Lew?

Lew Leone: Finally an easy question. Young Lew-Darren Criss. Present day Lew-Billy Bob Thornton.

Chris Dessi: Best day of your life?

Lew Leone: Wedding Day. Vero Beach Fl, morning golf tournament and " The Land Sharks" band

Chris Dessi: Worst day of your life?

Lew Leone: 9/11.

SPEED ROUND

Q. Mets or Yankees?

A. *Yankees.*

Q. Rosanna or Greg?

A. *I'm sure they would both love for me to answer that question.*

Q. Football or Baseball?

A. *Football.*

Q. Favorite Joke/Comedian?

A. *The Amazing Goldstein.*

Q. Favorite book?

A. *Still Life with Woodpecker.*

Q. Early bird or Night owl?

A. *Early Bird.*

Q. You and Greg Kelly get into a fistfight, who wins?

A. Well he is very stubborn so every time I knock him down he will always get up.

Q. Did Ernie really say what we think he said?

A. Yes, he said "Stay Classy New York."

Q. Beer or wine?

A. *Both.*

Q. My kids know that I hate witches, what's the one thing that scared the hell out of you as a kid, and still freaks you out?

A. *I don't like goodbyes and to this day I prefer just to disappear.*

Powerful Secrets to Success from a Marine

CHRIS MALONEY
U.S. Marine, Pilot, Co-founder at Cause Engine

My first "Success" interview ever was with Chris Maloney. I love this guy. Chris and I met when he interned for me. Chris is a military veteran. He's also an entrepreneur and reservist. Chris even invited me to speak about digital & social media to his colleagues at Stewart Air National Guard Base. Chris has helped Silverback Social work on social media campaigns. He also worked with us on last year's Westchester Digital Summit. I consider Chris a huge success. I should have been paying him to consult for me rather than have him intern. He wanted to learn about digital marketing. So he took an unpaid internship to immerse himself in our industry. He taught me more about operations and how to run my agency than I could ever teach him. He's also a great guy and a great friend. Here we go.

Chris Dessi: Chris, when we first met you were spending weekends flying missions for the US military. You were also spending alternating off weekends down at the New Jersey shore helping your Dad renovate your hotel. You found time to work on your MBA at Fordham University as well. All this while being one of most valuable employees at Silverback. How do you manage it all? Do you have a secret regarding your time management?

Chris Maloney: I'm better giving time management advice than heeding it. I'm a habitual procrastinator and try to fill my schedule and take on as many tasks to avoid the creep of laziness. The past two years in NYC have been a sort whack-a-mole of missions, mostly self-generated,  to figure out what the next chapter would be after about ten years active duty in the Marine Corps. When I find work quality degrading, I know it's time to stop, reprioritize, and cut whatever excess exists — then re-attack. Since my time at Silverback, I've throttled back on motel operations and my Dad continues to run the show down in Strathmere, NJ. I was doing too much last year with a full-time MBA, internships, trying to run a veterans organization at Fordham, revive an old American Legion in Greenwich Village, and fulfill my commitment to the

Marine Corps reserves. Right now I'm focusing on my last two MBA classes, the reserves, andmostly CauseEngine, a company I co-founded that connects talented freelancers to nonprofits to drive operations and social impact. OPEN was one acronym I took on last year. I asked Gerry Byrne, a Fordham Alumni, Marine Vietnam Veteran, and former publisher of Variety magazine, almost the same question you're asking me. He said to OPEN your day: Organize, Prioritize, Execute, and Navigate.

Chris Dessi: I have a tremendous amount of respect for the military. I was even more impressed when I met the men and women that you serve with. What do you think about on Memorial Day? Like, is it a profound day of introspection for you? Or are you spending the day out and about experiencing as much as you can in this great country of ours?

Chris Maloney: I've noticed many servicemen and women that get bent out of shape because the majority of America doesn't know the meaning of Memorial Day. I get it, but I don't subscribe to the "I'm a veteran, hear me roar" mindset. Besides heading to veterans' cemeteries with my Dad when I was younger, I didn't have a clue either. It wasn't until I went to the Naval Academy and then served and deployed a few times that I really grasped the meaning of the day. To be honest, every day is Memorial Day for me now. Not a day goes by that I don't think about the likes of Michael LiCalzi, Travis Manion, Brendan Looney (this list could go on for awhile) and attempt to live my life reaching for the standard they set. The official day is more a tip of the cap for me, acknowledging those men and women that stepped into the arena and laid it all out for their country and more importantly, their brothers and sisters serving beside them. My introspection is also directly proportional to my alcohol consumption! America was, is, and will be in good hands — for that I'm grateful, and hope our citizens are too.

Chris Dessi: During your tenure at Silverback you had a harrowing experience when lightening hit your plane. What was that like? Did your training kick in, or did you have a true "oh shit, I'm a deadman" thought?

Chris Maloney: A little lightening was no big deal! I'm kidding. I was scared shitless. My thought process: Did that just happen? (That's never happened before.) Am I alive? Yes. Are we in the air? Yes. Is the aircraft flying the way it should be? Yes. Are we on fire? No. Ok.

We need to land now. Luckily I was in the plane with some very experienced Marines and crew-members and landed safely without an issue.

Chris Dessi: I'm obsessed with CrossFit. It changed my body. I also feel like I need to work out to be successful. I have a clear mind and feel more focused after I work out. How much does your fitness regiment contribute to your success?

Chris Maloney: I'm like the Irish guy in the movie Braveheart when I don't workout — "not right in the head." I can't focus. I really think when you work out in the morning you set the tone for the day. We are meant to move. I don't belong to a CrossFit gym but think the workouts are the best around.

Chris Dessi: Why the military? What got you there? Are you from a military family? Were you affected by September 11th? I'm so curious what draws guys like you to service? What's your journey been like?

Chris Maloney: Those are some big questions. My Dad served over 30 years in the Marine Corps. He was a helicopter pilot, flew President Reagan and was the Commanding Officer of a squadron as a reservist. As a little kid, I wanted to be like him and his fellow Marines. I sometimes  forget that my Mom was an Air Force nurse for a few years too. I think she outranked him when they met. Both my grandfathers served in the Navy and Air Force as well so, yes, I guess you could say I come from a military family, but it was never forced on us growing up. My journey in a few sentences: I received a commission in the Marine Corps after graduation and began bouncing around the country training to be a pilot. For the most part, I was based out of San Diego and ended up deploying to Iraq once and

Afghanistan three times. I did one tour on the ground with the infantry, serving as a Forward Air Controller — the guy who calls in air strikes or medevac flights. 9/11 served and still

serves as a reminder of why we do what we do.

Chris Dessi: You've seen military success. Now business success. What do you consider your biggest success thus far? What else do you want to do?

Chris Maloney: Biggest success was playing a small part in helping everyone in our company (Kilo Company, 3rdBattalion 7th Marines) come home alive from Afghanistan in 2010. We were blessed with some incredible leadership and some very aggressive, but smart, Marines and Sailors.

Chris and My Daughters

I'd like to have an impact wherever I go. Right now that means building out the CauseEngine brand and platform. I'd love to see this company take off and be the single source powering the social sector — giving professionals and freelancers an outlet to use their skills doing good (and getting paid) and giving nonprofits a place to find on-demand talent to grow their impact and cause.

Chris Dessi: You run a hotel with your Dad, you have a business partner. You're doing lots of entrepreneurial work. What's that been like? Do you see yourself continuing to create businesses with Dad? Has that been difficult?

Chris Maloney: My Dad and I are pretty stubborn, and that sometimes leads to an Irish Marine standoff and not a lot of communication. Like I said, I'm passively involved right now. I think doing business with family always has risks, but I wouldn't make the blanket statement that people should never do business with family or friends. I'm one of three founders at CauseEngine and the managing director, James Brobyn, was my college roommate. We never worked with each other, so it's been a learning experience, especially operating remotely. James is in Wilmington, DE, and Mackenzie Padell is in Virginia Beach, VA. We are finally grabbing an office space in Philly, so that is exciting and will change the dynamic. To note, both James and Mac are former successful executive directors and incredible humans. If you want to support some high impact veteran organizations, check out the Travis Manion Foundation and 31 Heroes Project when you have a chance.

Chris Dessi: You're presented with stressful situations while on military missions. How do you cope? Do you meditate? How do you define "down time." Does that mean time with family, or does that just mean beers with the guys. How do you unwind?

Chris Maloney: Easier said than done, but leave the emotions out of it, operate like a surgeon, and deal with the feelings after the mission. I'm Catholic but not a Bible thumper. For me, attending Mass is a good place to center my chi and have some quiet time. I try to go every week. My family and friends are unbelievably supportive and a big part of why I moved back to the east coast. I like to carpe as much diem as I can during my down time, and there's always something to do in NYC and Philly.

Chris Dessi: Best day of your life?

Chris Maloney: October 14, 2010.

Chris Dessi: Worst day of your life?

Chris Maloney: October 14, 2010.

Chris Dessi: Those who read my blog know that my Father has been a huge influence on my life. Is there someone in your life that had helped to define the man you've become?

Chris Maloney: Both my parents. My Dad is your old school, no BS, mission-oriented, workaholic and my Mom should be nominated for sainthood. She's the glue and does everything for our family. Both have huge hearts, and I've learned equally from them. Besides my parents I think many of my coaches and fellow Marines helped define who I am. As a kid, I loved Murdock from the "A-Team" and Baloo from the cartoon "Tailspin."

Chris Dessi: What's your daily routine. What time do you usually go to bed? What time do you rise?

Chris Maloney: Usually in bed by midnight and up by 7 am but some-times I don't have a choice when my moti-vated girlfriend gets up at 5 am.

Chris Dessi: How do you define success? How much does luck account for your successes in life?

Chris Maloney: For me success is making a difference in the world or someone's life. Luck is when preparation meets opportunity. I'd like to be successfully lucky. I have no idea what I just said! Just be a good person. Stand up for what is right. Give the fucks. If you care enough about something or somebody, you'll find the right opportunity and make luck happen. If it doesn't happen, take a breath, maybe a Jameson, and try harder. Put the left in front of the right, keep moving, and occasionally give high fives to people you don't know. Enjoy it all and don't stop believing. That's success!

SPEED ROUND

Q. God Bless America, or The Star Spangled Banner?

A. Star Spangled Banner — the lyrics and the context are pretty awesome.

Q. My daughters know that I hate witches. What (if anything) used the scare the hell out of you as a kid?

A. The Jersey Devil. Google this thing. I swear it was in our backyard when I was growing up.

Q. Do you have a saying that is your life motto?

A. I'm a pretty big Teddy Roosevelt and MLK fan. "Injustice anywhere is a threat to justice everywhere." —MLK

"Get action. Do things; be sane; don't fritter away your time; create, act, take a place wherever you are and be somebody; get action." —Teddy Roosevelt

Two of my own: "Always the people, never the place.", "Home is where the fart is."

Q. What keeps you up at night?

A. Coffee from my 8-10pm classes and not amounting to anything.

Q. When did you consider yourself a success?

A. I don't yet, but I think having a family would change that.

Q. Rap or Rock and Roll?

A. Rock and Roll. Most music these days is mindless crap.

Q. Stick shift or automatic?

A. Automatic. Smarter, not harder.

Q. Muscle Car or Italian Sports Car?

A. Muscle car.

Q. Hulk Hogan or Rowdy Roddy Piper?

A. Hulkster. The Ultimate Warrior and the Bushwackers were pretty cool too.

A New Generation CEO Who's Blazing His Own Path to Success

TODD MARKS
CEO, President, and Founder Mindgrub

It was a hot day in the Spring of 1995. We had just completed a grueling Rugby practice at Loyola University, Maryland. In reality, every Rugby practice was grueling for me. I wasn't a good player. I didn't know the rules well. I think I scored once. I was slow. I even broke my nose while playing against the Naval Academy. My coach stuffed my nostrils with cloth and pushed me back on the pitch. I just wanted to drink beer and meet girls.

I suffered a few concussions on the Rugby pitch too. One concussion was so bad that I didn't recall driving home from a game. The 40 miles between the University of Maryland's campus and Loyola completely escaped me. But, I did know a few things. Rugby was fun. Rugby was social. *Girls liked Rugby players.* You got to drink beer after you played Rugby. So, I played Rugby. It worked. I met girls, made lifelong friends and enjoyed all that Rugby had to offer. Our best player was Sean Lugano. In fact, he was an All American. When Sean spoke, people listened. He was our surrogate coach most practices. Our "real" coach was a volunteer. I don't think they paid him well (if at all). He also had a real job. The result was that players organized practice. Players gave post-practice speeches. Players doled out discipline and praise when needed. The most commentary came from Sean. Less from other upper class men. I had never heard a Sophomore say a word in practice, let alone a Freshman. Which is why it was so odd on that hot day to hear from any player other than Sean.

He was a skinny redhead that flew under the radar. A nice kid for sure, but not one that you would expect to hear from at practice. We were all gathered around, waiting to hear from our captain Sean. Everyone took a knee. Sean stood in the center. We fell silent. Sean took a breath and looked like he was about to speak when he was interrupted. A voice broke the silence. "Fellas, remember to stay hydrated. You need to drink fluids after a practice like this. If you're not sure if you're fully hydrated, just take a look at your urine. Clear urine is good. Yellow urine is bad." Shocked into silence, we waited for Sean to explode. One beat, two beats. Sean looked around, and burst into laughter. Blurting out, "well, thanks for the tip, DOC!" Everyone laughed.

Sean said what he had to say, our practice ended, and we all went our separate ways. But something stuck. From that day forward my Rugby teammate, Todd Marks was known as "Doc."

A few years ago Doc and I reconnected. He was up in New York and thought it would be fun to say hello. It was. It's been fun to watch Todd's star rise. He's launched a successful agency and is bringing great pride to the Loyola Greyhound community. Todd is a 40 under 40, 2x EY Entrepreneur of the Year Nominee, and is the teacher-turned-technologist founder of Mindgrub Technologies. Mindgrub was voted CRTC's Tech Company of the Year and placed #520 on the Inc 500/5000. It's a mobile, social and web app consultancy, working with companies and organizations in a variety of industries to bring their brand to digital.

As you can tell by this story, Todd is a confident guy. He's continued to be confident throughout his career. He's built one of the most successful companies in Maryland. Which is why I thought he'll be the perfect candidate to profile in these success interviews. Please welcome, Todd "Doc" Marks.

Chris Dessi: What are some of the qualities that make for a great chief everything officer?

Todd Marks: As the Chief Everything Officer, I lead information architects, user experience specialists, creative interface designers, and top-notch developers to solve business and consumer challenges in application development and rapid prototyping. I grow new divisions of the business and hire and mentor staff to manage and grow those divisions. I lead and foster leadership within the organization.

Chris Dessi: You have a great entrepreneurial story. Eating Raman, riding your bike to work — during the more difficult times, before things took off, how did you keep a positive mindset and continue to push forward.

Todd Marks: I kept a positive outlook out of sheer necessity. I had gone too far down the rapid path to fail. I would have been out on the street if Mindgrub wasn't successful, so there was no alternative than always to think positively and put my best foot forward every day.

Chris Dessi: When Apple release the iPhone you saw disruption and jumped on it. Throughout history, some of the most successful entrepreneurs from Rockefeller and Carnegie to Jobs have followed that model. What current disruptions do you see here or coming next and how do you develop the confidence to jump on the opportunity?

Todd Marks: The current disruptions I see are health tech, the gamification of learning, hyperlocal location, wayfinding, location-based messaging, and virtual reality.

When you're climbing a cliff, you want to always use a safety rope. So when you're jumping on one of these disruptions, it's an opportunity that you want to come into safely and at the right time. Venture into a disruption, but make sure you're not getting in too early too fast, and you're not overspending in the market too early.

Chris Dessi: It appears you like to give back. You teach

a course at UMBC and sit on the advisory board for two organizations. Given your already busy schedule, how do you evaluate which additional obligations you add to your plate?

Todd Marks: My schedule is always full, but I'm committed to supporting the local tech community. So that's why I work with organizations where I can make a meaningful impact with a small time commitment.

Chris Dessi: How important are habits and routine to your success?

Todd Marks: Routine is very important to me. I'm extremely habitual.

Chris Dessi: What is your Rhythm?

Todd Marks: I'm always on and working from early in the morning until I go to bed, but when I relax, I really relax.

Chris Dessi: What time do you go to bed?

Todd Marks: I'm usually in bed by 9 pm on school nights, and 10 pm on weekend nights. But I'm always up by 3 or 4 am.

Chris Dessi: Do you meditate?

Todd Marks: In my own way, yes.

Chris Dessi: For people like yourself who have seen great monetary success — what do you think is dangerous about that type of success?

Todd Marks: I don't think I've received great monetary success. Maybe if I sold the company, but for now I think I earn a pretty meager salary. That being said, the danger you run into when bringing in a lot of revenue with your business is that you assume a lot of financial obligations. At some point, you might burn through your savings or not save while your expenses exceed your cash flow. If you can't cut those expenses off fast enough, you get into a cash crunch or serious debt you can't recover from. That is dangerous.

Chris Dessi: I speak with many successful executives that question the value of college. Since we both attended Loyola University in Maryland — What do you say to those detractors of education?

Todd Marks: At 18-21 years old, you're still coming into your own. College provides structure for children maturing into adults, and it provides a good network of friends and colleagues. I do think that there are other ways to get that same structure independent of college. I'm not saying that you don't need college, but I am saying that if you can get the same structure and network, plus have the discipline for self-learning, I don't know that you need college. Though, it is an exception more than the norm in this day and age.

Chris Dessi: How do you define success?

Todd Marks: Success is reaching your goals, and feeling a sense of accomplishment.

Chris Dessi: Can you explain the impact, that social networking/digital media has made on your business/career or you personally?

Todd Marks: Early on, social media allowed Mindgrub to market our brand cheaply, and bootstrap our business without having a lot of upfront funding.

Chris Dessi: How much of your success was due to luck? Or are you of the mindset that you create your luck?

Todd Marks: I have no luck. None of my success is due to luck. It's due to building enough experience, finding a need in the market, and coming in at the right time during a disruption.

Chris Dessi: When did you first think of yourselves as a success?

Todd Marks: I don't view myself as a success. Others may view me that way, but I'm just doing my thing.

Chris Dessi: Many young executive who read my blog struggle with work life/balance — myself included. What advice do you give them? How do you each strike a balance?

Todd Marks: My advice is to find a worthy distraction from your work. Get a partner, kids, or a hobby that will make you want to spend a lot of time away from work. If you're working like a dog, in an unhealthy way, then you haven't found the right distractions.

Chris Dessi: On paper your resumes reads like success. Can you tell us about your biggest failure(s)? How did it change you or shift your approach moving forward?

Todd Marks:: I don't view anything I have done as a failure. Anything that wasn't as successful as I wanted it to be was still a learning opportunity. Failure has zero positive outcomes that I haven't encountered and which I don't like to dwell on.

Chris Dessi: Who has been the greatest positive influence on your life? Tell us about that person.

Todd Marks: My fiancee has been the greatest positive influence on my life. She's also an entrepreneur, owns several businesses, and she's created a great sense of family that was lacking before in previous relationships.

Chris Dessi: What do you think is the one characteristic that all the successful people you know share?

Todd Marks: High intelligence and street smarts.

Chris Dessi: How has your childhood (the way you were raised, your birth order) affected your career success? Did it at all?

Todd Marks: I was the second child with an older sister. I did my own thing, and it gave me a great sense of independence.

Chris Dessi: I know you to be very humble people. Here is your chance to brag a bit — what has been your greatest career success to date?

Todd Marks: A combination of Mindgrub winning the Chesapeake Regional Tech Council's Tech Company of the Year, and being named one of Baltimore Magazine's Best Places to Work.

Chris Dessi: My daughters know that I hate witches — what's one thing that scares the hell out of you?

Todd Marks: Honestly, I'm not afraid of anything.

Chris Dessi: Best day of your life?

Todd Marks: When my fiancee said yes.

Chris Dessi: Worst day of your life?

Todd Marks: When I was robo-dialing friends and family to try to cover payroll in 2009 during the recession.

Chris Dessi: Who is your hero?

Todd Marks: I'm enamored of many people, but there's too many to name one hero.

Chris Dessi: What is the best gift you've ever been given?

Todd Marks: Homemade crafts from my daughters.

Chris Dessi: Do you collect anything?

Todd Marks: As a child I collected Star Wars Figures, Legos, Garbage Pail Kids, Cards, and Rocks. As an adult, I don't collect per se, but I do enjoy my tools, plants, sports equipment and outdoor gear.

Chris Dessi: What motivates you to work as hard as you do?

Todd Marks: I have a large blended family with seven kids, so putting a roof over nine heads is a real motivator.

Chris Dessi: Name someone who knows more about you than anyone else in the world.

Todd Marks: My fiancee.

Chris Dessi: Most powerful book you've ever read that you recommend to everyone?

Todd Marks: I don't often recommend books, but some books I enjoy include Outliers, Crossing the Chasm, Innovator's Dilemma, The Singularity is Near, and The Pleasure of Figuring Things Out.

A Wordsmith in His Prime

JEFF PEARLMAN
Best Selling Author

In the Spring of 1990, my big brother Mark was heading to Villanova University. Mark was in the final months of a fairly remarkable High School career. He was a member of the National Honor Society. He was a straight "A" student. He was also Captain of the Mahopac High School football team. Not an easy act to follow by any stretch of the imagination. One afternoon that Spring, Jeff Pearlman — a lanky classmate of my brothers — came to the house. Jeff was Editor-in-chief of the Mahopac Chieftain — the school paper. But that day was different. Jeff was there to interview my brother for a local "real" newspaper. Mark was considering walking onto the Villanova University Division 1AA football team. This was big news. Well, at least it was big news in our tiny town. I'll admit — it was exciting.

Jeff sat with my brother in his room to ask him a few questions. Like a good little brother, I crouched at the doorway and eavesdropped on every word. Jeff took some photos and ran the story. That visit to my home was the first real interaction I had with Jeff. Before that, I had seen him for sure, but being three years older, our social circles remained distant.

As years passed, I learned that Jeff was penning articles for Sports Illustrated. Mahopac watched as Jeff's star rose. Before long, he was writing New York Times best-selling sports biographies. Seeing Jeff's work in the local Barnes and Noble was a thrill. Later on we connected via social media. When I wanted to write a book of my own, I turned to Jeff to help edit and guide me. He even gave the book its title. Jeff asked that I speak to his journalism class at Manhattanville about social media. A real friendship was born.

My Father's ALS diagnosis hit my family hard. Like any other good friend, Jeff would check in from time to time. I'd get a message on Facebook at midnight. It was simple, to the point. "How's Dad?" Genuine. Caring. Selfless. Inquisitive. All the characteristics that make Jeff a phenomenal journalist were also characteristics that make him a great friend. Jeff once asked for my parent's address. I thought nothing of it at the time. Weeks later, my Dad bragged about the autographed books Jeff had sent.

Jeff has a section of his blog called the "Quaz." He calls it the "quirkiest, funkiest, Q&A series on the web." I'd agree. It's an insightful and wonderful piece of the internet that I never miss. A few years into Dad's battle with ALS, Jeff expressed an interest in featuring Dad. He agreed. The resulting interview shook my family to its core. Jeff captured the torture of ALS from a man living it. Dad shared things with Jeff that only his close family knew. Jeff honored my Father and produced (what has now become) a family treasure. When I decided to run the canceled New York City Marathon in my backyard to honor my Father, Jeff wrote about it on Sports Illustrated. Just weeks before my Father passed away, Jeff honored me and sent me questions so he could feature me in his "Quaz." Before I could answer the questions, Dad died. I completed my answers to Jeff's Quaz in the days following Dad's funeral. It was a welcomed distraction.

Jeff Pearlman has close ties to the Dessi family. We love Jeff. His Quaz inspired these "Success" interviews. Jeff is a great kid from the "mean streets of Mahopac." Jeff is also a huge success.

Let's do this.

Chris Dessi: How do you define success?

Jeff Pearlman: It's a funny question. Back when I was coming up, first at the University of Delaware, then at The Tennessean in Nashville, my answer would have been something like, "Making it to Sports Illustrated" or "having an SI cover story." Because, from the time I was in junior high, that was the dream — to write for SI. So success would be accomplishing my career dream. I mean, that's all I knew. I was a pretty shallow person who aspired—more than anything—to be a famous writer.

And, while I've loved my career, what passed for "success" at 23, 24, 25 doesn't hold an ounce of weight now, at 43. I mean, it's laughable, and I feel bad for people who have this measure of success, via fame or money or title. And I look back with a little bit of shame (actually, a lot of shame), because in pursuing my vision of success I was, quite often, an arrogant, dismissive, listen-to-nobody dickwad of the first degree. I was so absorbed in the pursuit of what I considered to be greatness that I failed in 800 different measures of decency.

This is a long-winded answer to a basic request. For me, at 43, success means that tomorrow I'll drop my son off at school, then return 20 minutes later to help the class with Friday morning spelling. It means rarely (almost never) missing a Little League game, a concert, a water polo meet, a play. It means knowing all my kids' friends, making lunches in the morning, putting them to bed at night. And it's weird because the dickwad me of 24 sort of made it possible at 43 to have this life of a work-from-home (or the nearest coffee shop) writer. So I have to accept that.

But success, truly, is being an involved dad.

Chris Dessi: Your books largely follow successful (albeit in some cases controversial athletes) what pieces of success were you able to pick up from them if any?

Jeff Pearlman: Well, here's the catch: Sports success vs. life success — it's a TOTALLY different thing. In sports, to be great, you sorta kinda, kinda sorta, have to be a selfish prick. It's weird, right? But the greatest athletes I've covered have — me when it comes to letting others in on their success secrets (generally, they don't share much information), when it comes to contract negotiations. I've had this discussion with tons of high-level jocks, and — rarely by name — they admit it's not first and foremost about the team. It's about the contract, the endorsements, the headlines. Because, a lot of these guys either come from rural bumblefuck or the rough inner-cities. While it's nice to say, "I'm all about helping the Chiefs win the Super Bowl," the first priority is making as much coin as humanly possible in the short window that is your athletic career. And if you win, terrific. But if you don't, generally, it's digestible.

One guy I really studied, in this regard, was Barry Bonds. Forget the cheating for a minute. Bonds was as hyper-focused as any athlete I've ever seen. Everything he did in his life was about hitting baseballs over walls. It was crazy to watch. I mean, obsession times 100,000. And he wasn't doing it so the Giants would win. He was doing it to hit 50-plus home runs, so the team would pay him and companies would endorse him. That way, his family would be set for eons. It ain't sexy. But it's reality.

Chris Dessi: You've talked about "hurting for journalism." What advice do you have for today's students and young professionals who have a passion for journalism? Any tips on how they can succeed today?

Jeff Pearlman: It's a much more confusing ballgame than when I entered the workforce in 1994. Back then, the path for folks like me, Jon Wertheim, Grant Wahl, Howard Bryant, Jonathan Eig, name young sports writers from the time period, and we all knew we had to probably start at a newspaper. Then, (if it's what you wanted) get hired by a magazine. That was the path—period. No Web, no Twitter, etc. But now, I don't think many journalism students think, "I can't wait to write for a newspaper!" I mean, jobs are dropping every other day, and who under the age of 30 even picks up a paper? It's sad. That being said, there are more avenues than ever. I mean, sooooo many more, which is exciting. So how do you wind up at a good one that pays well? As far as I can tell, you do what has always been done by top-shelf writers. You outwork and out-write the competition. You find creative angles and ideas nobody else thinks of. You pitch everywhere.

I'm not saying I'm anything special—because, truly, I'm not. But back when I was coming up at SI, I was a reporter (aka fact checker). We worked four days per week, which was sweet. Well, on at least one or two off days every week, I'd go to the office, close the door and call college sports information director after college sports information director, begging for unique/cool/funky story ideas. Before long, I had dozens upon dozens of them—and it's how I got into the magazine so often. Was I a better writer than my peers? No. Did I have a talent they lacked? No. I just r-e-a-l-l-y wanted it, as badly as I wanted anything. So I busted my ass. That's the secret to success that's not really a secret: Busting your ass improves your odds dramatically.

Chris Dessi: In a lot of ways your website/blog were ahead of its time. They are gritty, raw, honest and personal. On the one hand — today success is tied with transparency. On the other hand — we live in a hypercritical world. Talk about your mindset to use your blog as this personal forum and also a little bit about how you deal with backlash on some of the more controversial issues you cover.

Jeff Pearlman: I started the blog in 2008, sort of as a lark. Or, really, a vent; a chance to blather on about stuff. That was really it. But slowly, over the years, I've gained a bit of a following. Which is weird, but not weird. Weird, because I've blogged about everything from blood in my poop to a wrist wart that won't go away to my Hall and Oates and Blind Melon obsessions. There's nothing especially news-breaking or earth-shattering. But it's not weird because I think people dig the honesty and the funny little stories. My wife is a fan of reality TV. Not because it's good programing, but because it's an escape. Sometimes it's nice to see what other people are doing to take the mind off your own life. Maybe that's the secret to my website's mediocre, have-never-made-a-cent-off-of-it reception. One more thing: Being an unaffiliated sports writer allows me to do things Jemele Hill and Tom Verducci and most others in the biz can't: Namely, critique the media. I have no corporate ties; jeffpearlman.com isn't also an NFL rights holder. I can slam Jason Whitlock or Mike Lupica when they're being arrogant asswipes, and the only blow-back might be an angry e-mail. It's ridiculously liberating. And fun. I never thought I'd enjoy blogging as much as I do. And, again, it has zero to do with the money. Because the pay is entertainment, and a chance to blog about Mr. T and Emmanuel Lewis and John Oates and the Alf puppet as often as I'd like.

Chris Dessi: Can you explain the impact, that social networking/digital media has made on your business/career or you personally?

Jeff Pearlman: It's very love-hate for me. So, as a guy who makes his living writing books, I need to be pretty active on social media. I need Twitter followers, Facebook friends. Because I need to show publishing companies I have a built-in following who will, hopefully, both spread word of a new book and buy it. Really, I've become a complete and total social media whore—with one eye always on building up as big a following as possible.

That being said, well, I love it. I do. Writing can be terribly lonely and isolating. There's an amazing writer named Leigh Montville, and he once said something I've never forgotten: "A career writing books is like living in a cave for two years, popping your head into the sun for a week or two, then returning to the cave." It's perfectly said, because save for the short period of post-release sunlight, you're a hermit. Twitter and Facebook—they connect me to people. I'll do "Ask me anything you want" sessions on Twitter, get a few hundred questions about writing, and laugh when people thank me for their time. Thank me? Hell, thank you. You're keeping me sane.

Chris Dessi: How much of your success was due to luck? Or are you of the mindset that you create your luck?

Jeff Pearlman: It's funny. There's this whole debate going on about immigration in this country, and you have these self-righteous so-called patriots all but throwing rocks at illegal immigrants trying to live here. And you know why—99.9% of the time—the self-righteous so-called patriots live here? Womb placement. Seriously. They were born here because the woman who carried them in the womb was standing on American soil. THAT'S luck.

Am I lucky? Hell, yes. I was born to two amazing, supportive parents who paid for my college education. Who allowed me to take their car to Urbana, Illinois in the summer of 1992 so I could intern at a newspaper for $5 an hour. Who bought me a used car so I could spend the following summer interning in Nashville. Parents Who listened (or, perhaps, pretended to listen) as I read every high school newspaper story aloud on their bed. Who encouraged me to pursue my dream. Who raised me to be *open-minded* and to seek*adventure*. Yeah, you create your own luck by working hard and making contacts. But my life, truly, is a joke. So many people in this world struggle in so many different ways. And, for no good reason, I've lived this blessed, charmed existence. I'm no more worthy than the 43-year-old Syrian refugee. Crap, I'm 8,000 times less worthy. But I'm here, sipping a cup of coffee at my kitchen table, my kids asleep upstairs. And he's a refugee. It makes no sense.

Chris Dessi: If you could wave a magic wand, and change one thing about journalism — what would it be?

Jeff Pearlman: Speaking primarily (but not exclusively) of sports television, I would blow up the way networks treat women reporters. It's disgraceful. Men can look like lumpy plates of tuna casserole and last in front of the camera into their 60s, 70s. If women don't look like Erin Andrews, their odds of getting a prime gig on a huge network are, sadly, slim. And it's a repugnant reality.

Chris Dessi: Your books have become legendary for their exhaustive research — what's your process? Or do you not have one — just diving in and going for it?

Jeff Pearlman: I appreciate the kind words, but "legend-ary" is probably a stretch.

A long time ago, when I was coming up, I read an inter-view with Gary Smith, the fantastic former SI writer. And he spoke of always making the extra call. I'd never thought of it as such. Hell, at the time I was a pretty lazy reporter. But the idea stuck, and now—when I write a book—I'm all about making the extra call, and the extra call, and the extra call. Take "Sweetness," my Walter Payton biography, for example. The first thing I did was find all the old year-books and media guides he appeared in. I'd go through them, page by page by page, and make a Word file for everyone. Not just the stars. E-v-e-r-y-o-n-e. Every trainer, ball boy, draft pick, rookie free agent, coach, reception-ist. And then, well, I call. And call. And call. I have this guiding principle, and it's based around an experience I had in high school with a guy named Dave Fleming, who came out of Mahopac to wind up pitching for the Seattle Mariners. Dave lived about a half mile up the street from me, but we didn't know one another. When he was a senior, I was a freshman, and one day he happened to be on the school bus (maybe his car was in the shop). I was talking to a kid named Scott, and I asked him a trivia question—"Who was the leading rusher for the Los Angeles Rams in the Super Bowl?" And Dave turned around and said, "Wendell Tyler." OK, does Dave Fleming remember that moment? No way in hell. But I do, because he was THE Dave Fleming. That's how I think of these books. Were he alive, Walter Payton wouldn't remember the 1978 free agent safety from Bucknell. But the free agent safety from Bucknell will remember being in camp with Walter Payton. And he'll likely have a story or two.

That's why I call everyone.

Chris Dessi: How important are habits and routine to your success? What is your Rhythm? What time do you go to bed? Do you meditate?

Jeff Pearlman: I've never meditated, I probably get five hours of sleep most nights, I can't run any longer because of disc damage in my back. But what I love—like, love, love, love—is the coffee shop. The rhythms and sounds and buzz. I mean, it's my happy place. So often, when I'm writing, that's where you'll find me. Corner table, earplugs in (but usually no music), a cup of some overpriced nonsense by my side. I struggle writing in quiet isolation. I need people and the illusion of social interaction.

Chris Dessi: I speak with many successful executives that question the value of college. You have a degree from the University of Delaware, and you've been a college professor. What do you say to those detractors of education?

Jeff Pearlman: Well, I think colleges and universities are ludicrously overpriced, and it sucks that hundreds of thousands of Americans will be buried beneath college loan debt for years to come. It's a gross system, and for some the question truly can be asked, "Is this worth it? Is it worth attending college if I'll be paying it off until I'm 50?"

For me, it was beyond invaluable. Some of the greatest learning experiences of my life came at The Review, Delaware's student newspaper. I made tons of mistakes; got fired, got brought back; was threatened  with a lawsuit via an angry fraternity member; became editor in chief. There's no way I enjoy this career without having spent long hours eating greasy pizza in the Review offices. So, as far as journalism goes, it's pretty vital.

Chris Dessi: The first time I sat up and took notice of your career was when I read the John Rocker article. When did you first think of yourself as a success?

Jeff Pearlman: I'm not trying to sound modest, but my brain doesn't work in those terms. I've got a lot of my dad in me. He owned his own executive search firm for years; had a great career. But I don't think he ever settled; I think he always worried about what was coming, and why everything was about to collapse. It's probably not such a great thing, but I have that in me, too. I'm always thinking what's next, how can I survive, how can I make it and continue to write. Some people seem to think of themselves as stars. I don't. I mean, not even close. Even when I got hired at SI in 1996. It was the fruition of a dream—but I didn't consider myself as "a success." I thought of myself as a guy who now has to prove himself to a whole bunch of editors.

Chris Dessi: Many young executives who read this blog struggle with work life/balance. You always put your family first. Taking them to school, getting very involved in their activities and sports, etc. How do you strike a balance?

Jeff Pearlman: Well, I'm married to the greatest mother in America. Not just saying that—she's insane, and she's taught me an infinite amount about parenting, raising kids, maintaining the balance, etc. So that's huge.

One thing is, I'm very motivated by death. It's nothing to brag about, but it's true. I think about death every … single … day. How my time is tick-tick-ticking away. I'm very aware of it, RE: my kids, and how fast they're growing. I'm incredibly proud but also sad. My daughter is halfway to 24 — that blows my mind. So I'm hugely motivated by time, and not missing things. I think I have this belief that, if you're around as much as possible, the clock moves just a tiny bit slower.

Chris Dessi: Who has been the greatest positive influence on your professional life? Tell us about that person.

Jeff Pearlman: I'm a bit of a broken record on this, but my dad. Truly. So here's an example: Back in 1986, my dad wrote and self-published a business book called "Conquering the Corporate Career." It was terrific, and he printed up, oh, 1,000 copies, and I remember being so dazzled; so proud. One day we delivered a bunch of copies to the Waldenbooks in the Jefferson Valley Mall. I mean, MY dad had a book on the shelves in a huge store. We'd sneak in from time to time (OK, all the time) and move "Conquering the Corporate Career" from the business section to the best-seller's section—something I still do today with my books.

I used to think of my dad as Clark Kent and Superman. At home, he was Clark Kent. Un-athletic, not a good dresser, couldn't cook, etc. I mean, tremendous dad. But … Kent. Then, come Monday morning, I'd sit on the bed and watch him put his suit on. Then the tie. And he was fucking Superman. Sometimes my brother and I would go to his office, and he was The Man. It was his company. I can't tell you the impact that had on me. He had a dream, pursued it, achieved it.

Chris Dessi: What do you think is the one characteristic that all the successful people you know share?

Jeff Pearlman: I don't see it. Success is just a varied ideal. Is the sanitation worker successful if he loves his job? Yes. Is the miserable hedge fund trader successful if he comes home at 8 every night and his kids greet him with a hug? Yes. Is the baker who never wanted kids successful if he makes the best muffins in Tulsa? Yes. I think it's too simple to have "success" as this singular ideal or concept because we all have different definitions. Some would look at me (and you) and say "That's a successful guy," others would say, "total flop."

One thing I will say is this: The image of success is, often, bullshit, and harmful. When we look at others and say, "Man, if only I had that life …" we're fooling ourselves. I've known many famous, rich, family-oriented people who were miserable. And I know a whole bunch of low-paid, unrecognized working stiffs who walk with a kick in their step.

Chris Dessi: As a Jewish journalist — have you ever experienced discrimination in the workplace? How has that affected your outlook, and drive to succeed?

Jeff Pearlman: Honestly, I haven't had any issues. There are so many of us; it's not like anyone's discriminating.

Chris Dessi: You recently moved to LA from NY. How much of that decision was based on your career? Or was it more of a "hey, why not?" move?

Jeff Pearlman: It had zero to do with career, 100 percent to do with the brevity of life. I've never wanted to be the person who spends his time in one place, forever. We lived in New Rochelle, N. Y. for 11 terrific years. Great friends, amazing neighbors, ties that will last. I mean, it's as good a place to live as I know. But … personally, it was starting to feel stale. Repetitive. Did we do that thing two years ago, or four? Or five? Remember the party we had in 2009? Or was it 2011? Stuff blended.

So I'd spent much time in Southern Cal, both for my Lakers book, Showtime, and doing Jim Rome's show. And I loved it. The beach, the atmosphere. Everything. And I kept bugging Catherine, bugging her, bugging her. We even came out, and she liked it. Well, two years ago she was away for our wedding anniversary, but she left me a gift. And it was an old-school California Angels cap, with a note saying, "I'm scared, I'm nervous — but I'm in."

Great wife.

Chris Dessi: You seem to have perfected the art of self-deprecation on your blog — but here is your chance to brag a bit — what has been your greatest career success to date?

Jeff Pearlman: Chris, I never wear shoes. Seriously, never. It's flip-flops about 350 days a year. And shorts—basketball shorts usually. And ratty T-shirts. It's friggin' sweet. Awards mean nothing to me. Like, less than nothing. I don't care about being the best writer, or the best thing. I want happiness. And, for the most part, I've got it. That's my greatest career success. Truly.

RAPID FIRE

Chris Dessi: My daughters know that I hate witches — what's one thing that scares the hell out of you?

Jeff Pearlman: Whitewater rafting. Back in 1994 I had a truly terrifying experience, and I've never gone back.

Chris Dessi: Best day of your life?

Jeff Pearlman: Every Halloween.

Chris Dessi: Worst day of your life?

Jeff Pearlman: 9. 11. 2001—no close second.

Chris Dessi: Who is your hero?

Jeff Pearlman: My parents, Stan and Joan Pearlman

Chris Dessi: Oddest place you've been recognized?

Jeff Pearlman: I was taking the subway in New York, and I was on an escalator going down with my son; on the other side a guy was going up, and he said, "Hey, you're Jeff Pearlman!" It was weird because I have a contentedly anonymous life.

Chris Dessi: What motivates you to work as hard as you do?

Jeff Pearlman: The love of doing it.

Chris Dessi: Name someone who knows more about you than anyone else in the world:

Jeff Pearlman: Catherine Pearlman, my wife

Chris Dessi: Most powerful book you've ever read that you recommend to everyone (other than the ones you've written)?

Jeff Pearlman: The Autobiography of Malcolm X. I read it when I was 18, a Sheltered kid from a small town. Then—BOOM!

Success Secrets from America's Doctor

ROSHINI RAJ, MD
Medical Host, Author, Co-Founder of TULA

I'm lucky. I get to <u>go on TV</u> from time to time and meet amazing people. One of those people is Dr. Roshini Raj. I met Dr. Raj while on the Good Day New York set. She was curious about social media and asked if I could help her. A few weeks later, I met with her at her office in New York City, and we became friends. She's a powerhouse. She has an Ivy League education and movie star good looks.

She's a mother of two and a gastroenterologist. She's also a media correspondent, and recently she launched her skin-care brand, called TULA. Yep — Dr. Roshini Raj is a *total badass*. She's the embodiment of what I wish for my daughters. She has a career she loves, a supportive husband, two great kids, and an entrepreneurial spirit. She's got "success" written all over her. Asking her to answer a few questions for my success feature was a v-e-r-y easy decision. Read on to learn more about the powerhouse that is Dr. Roshini Raj.

Chris Dessi: We met because of your regular television appearances. What has led you there? How were you "discovered" or was this an intentional career path for you?

Roshini Raj MD: Although I always loved public speaking and gave regular lectures to the community on health topics, the television work did start somewhat randomly. A TV show came to my hospital (NYU) wanted to film a piece on colonoscopy and colon cancer screening. They wanted to film a female gastroenterologist so by default (there were hardly any of us) I was chosen to do it. After that, I was hooked! I loved the experience of communicating an educational message to so many people at once; and I felt very natural on camera. The producers thought I did a good job, and one thing lead to another after that.

Chris Dessi: You're young, you're beautiful, and you're a doctor. You're also a successful mother of two. I know this question may seem cliche', but I'm genuinely curious — how do you do it all? Do you have help? What role does your husband play at home?

Roshini Raj MD: I have tons of help, and I am not afraid to ask for more. I think a mistake many women make is feeling like they have to do everything themselves. Support is key, and I am very lucky to have an incredibly supportive husband. He is always happy to watch the kids if I have an early morning shoot or have to travel for work. Our babysitter is also amazing, and my parents live nearby and help a lot too. My mother always worked (she is a doctor) and my father (also a doctor) was a very hands-on Dad so I had great role models growing up in how a man and woman can be truly equal partners.

Chris Dessi: When was the first time you felt you were a success?

Roshini Raj MD: In terms of my media career, my first time on Today show was pretty incredible. I had dreamed of being on the show. It was every bit exciting as I thought it would be. In terms of my medical career, I have so many interactions during the day with my patients that make me feel like a "success." Whether I diagnosed the right condition, or simply make them feel better my listening, that human connection is very meaningful.

Chris Dessi: You strike me as the type of person that knew she was going to be in the medical field very early on. Am I totally off base here, or do you feel medicine was a calling?

Roshini Raj MD: Yes I did. Although both my parents are doctors, they never pressured me to go into medicine. But they did instill the value in me that whatever career I choose should be one that helps people. Seeing how much satisfaction they derived from their careers and the love and gratitude they received from patients inspired me to follow their footsteps.

Chris Dessi: A few weeks ago Kevin O'Leary from Shark Tank announced that his most profitable companies were all led by women. What do you think women business leaders do differently that you men can learn from?

Roshini Raj MD: Women are usually better listeners, we tend to be less arrogant, and we are great multi-taskers. (this makes me sound sexist, right?). SO while men tend to posture and sometimes act like they know something even if they don't, a woman will take the time to really investigate an issue, listen to the opinions of others, and a make a wise and careful decision.

Chris Dessi: How do you define success?

Roshini Raj MD: Success is when you derive joy from what you have and what you do. I am truly grateful for my family, career, and all that I have right now so in that sense I feel successful. But I still have many goals and ambitions I have yet to fulfill.

Chris Dessi: When I see women like you and my wife Laura — who work, and are active parents, I'm in awe. What (if any) role has your husband played in your success. I suppose I'm asking — how important has his support been for you?

Roshini Raj MD: His support has been essential. I could never do a last-minute TV spot at 5 AM or drop everything to fly to LA if my husband was not willing to pick up the slack at home. And on a daily basis he is a 50% (sometimes more) partner in raising our boys. I am lucky!!

Chris Dessi: I have two young daugh-ters. How important do you think it is for young women to see leaders like yourself in the news media, on TV and creating companies?

Roshini Raj MD: So important. As far as women have come we still have a long way to go regarding equal representation in leadership positions throughout every field. Seeing powerful women in the media and business world tells young girls that they should pursue their dreams no matter how lofty, and not let anything or anyone stand in their way.

Chris Dessi: You recently launched your health and beauty line called TULA. Tell me about the genesis of that launch? Has this always been a dream of yours, or was the business born from necessity.

Roshini Raj MD: Well as a 43-year-old woman, creating a powerful anti-aging skincare line was a bit of a necessity I suppose. But it was truly a labor of love. Being in the media, I love being able to help people live healthier lives, but I was ready to create a product that women can keep in their homes. I plan to expand TULA to a wellness brand that extends beyond skincare.

Chris Dessi: How great a role do you think luck has played in your success?

Roshini Raj MD: Luck has played a big role — specifically with chance encounters with people that became meaningful in my career. But on some level we create our own luck. Making sure you are in the right places at the right time helps a lot. You probably won't have a life-changing meeting if you stay at home all day.

Chris Dessi: You're a Medical Doctor — so you've taken academics seriously. What do you say to the pundits who feel that college is a waste of money?

Roshini Raj MD: I loved my college experience and felt that it made me a much more interesting person. I was an

English major (in addition to pre-med) and took so many fascinating courses in fields like film, ethnic conflict, and even opera. Most importantly I met wonderfully different people in college and my best friend today is my former college roommate.

Chris Dessi: Do you have brother and sisters? Where did you grow up? How has that shaped your successes?

Roshini Raj MD: I am an only child and grew up in Scarsdale, New York. Being an only child of working parents, I became very independent early on, and I still am. As busy as I am, I still crave some alone time every day — even just 15 minutes to maintain my sanity.

Chris Dessi: At first blush you seem to have it all. Loving family, new business, thriving medical practice, a book, and you're regularly on the most popular television shows. What has that journey been like? We know the highs — but tell me about the lows — where there bumps along the way?

Roshini Raj MD: Nobody's life is perfect. We all have lows

and challenges. I think being raised as a Buddhist has helped me cope with those challenges. In Buddhism, we acknowledge that life is full of suffering — whether it is illness, death, a breakup, divorce. Once you accept that some lows are inevitable, you learn to cope with them and focus on what is positive in your life. And I am very grateful that I have so many wonderful things in my life to focus on.

Chris Dessi: Are there women in your life who inspire your success? Tell me about them.

Roshini Raj MD: My mother for sure. She is a gastroenterologist running her own private practice, so she has certainly been a career role model. But she also lives life to the fullest — taking salsa lessons, learning about the latest tech gadgets, and having tons of fun.

Chris Dessi: What's your rhythm? What time do you go to bed? Do you meditate? If not — when and how do you find quiet time? When do you wake up? Do you exercise? If so — what do you do to keep fit?

Roshini Raj MD: I try to go to bed by 10 pm the latest and wake up at 6 am. I try to meditate daily but even if I don't get a chance to, I always take at least 15 minutes before bed to wind down. I exercise every day — I am basically addicted at this point. That hour in the gym is a form of relaxation for me.

Chris Dessi: Do you think there is room for a female Dr. Oz? (WINK WINK)

Roshini Raj MD: Absolutely!! Considering that women make most of the healthcare decisions in the household, we definitely need more women in the media that can speak to the female audience about health and wellness.

As much as I love Dr. Oz, there are some female-centric health topics that I think come best from a female doctor.

SPEED ROUND

Chris Dessi: Good Day New York or the Today Show?

Roshini Raj MD: Can't choose, love them both for different reasons.

Chris Dessi: My daughters know that I hate witches. What (if anything) used the scare the hell out of you as a kid?

Roshini Raj MD: Vans. I think I saw a movie about a child being kidnapped in a white van — so for years I would get scared when I saw one.

Chris Dessi: If you weren't a Doctor, what profession would you have chosen?

Roshini Raj MD: Honestly, I can't imagine doing anything else.

Chris Dessi: Best Pizza place in NYC?

Roshini Raj MD: Gigino's in Battery Park City.

Chris Dessi: Craziest place someone has recognized you?

Roshini Raj MD: Security line at the airport — they let me go through the fast lane!

Chris Dessi: Have you ever been in a car accident?

Roshini Raj MD: Knock on wood — never in a serious one. (weird question!)

Chris Dessi: What's the best advice you've ever received?

Roshini Raj MD: Don't let naysayers discourage you.

Chris Dessi: Do you have a life motto?

Roshini Raj MD: Look on the bright side.

Chris Dessi: What cheers you up?

Roshini Raj MD: hearing my kids laugh

Chris Dessi: What's your worst vice?

Roshini Raj MD: I love chocolate mousse. I don't indulge often but when I do — look out!

Chris Dessi: Arrive alive and drive 55, or are you a speed junky?

Roshini Raj MD: Ever since I had kids I am a very paranoid driver, so you will find me in the slow lane.

Learn more about Roshini Raj MD on her website, follow her on Twitter @DrRoshiniRaj, and join like-minded powerhouse professional women on her Facebook page https://www.facebook.com/DrRoshiniRaj

Take a look at her skincare line Tula: http://tulaforlife.com/

A Spectacular Succcess Forged by Unfathomable Tragedy

RAYMOND A. SANSEVERINO
Chair of Loeb & Loeb's Real Estate Department

My Sicilian Grandmother used to call me a "chiacchi-erone." Translated to English — it means *I talk a lot.* I think it's a good trait to be able to carry on a conversation with people from all walks of life. It's helped me in my career for sure. I can talk to anyone. I believe the best trait of a good conversationalist is someone who knows when it's time to shut up and listen. This can be a double-edged sword. I love listening when people have something to contribute. I loathe listening when people don't have anything to say. Seems obvious, but it's rare to find someone with something *truly* meaningful to contribute. Most talk is small. Most interactions are tertiary at best Passing interactions. How are the kids? How's the job? Are your parents doing well? Yada yada. This is when I zone out. My wife yells at me for it. She'll spot me across the room at parties and shout across the room. "CHRIS, STOP IT, YOU'RE EMBARRASSING ME." Not really, she just shoots me a look. If you're married, you know the look. I can hear her shouting at me in my head — so it's v-e-r-y real for me.

Jokes aside — I seek deep interaction. Don't we all? We all crave thoughtful people and compelling conversation in our lives. People with something to *contribute*.

A few months ago, in an unlikely place, on a normal Sunday, I had a profound conversation that shook me to my core. I was in the car with my daughter Talia, her classmate Sophie, and Sophie's Dad, Ray. Ray had invited us to join them for a New Jersey Devil's game. Ray has season tickets and thought it would be a great way for the girls to enjoy the sport. Ray and I didn't know each other well at the time. We maybe had two conversations before that car ride. The first time we spoke was at Ray's home. He and his wife Kimber threw a pool party for the girls' first-grade class, and their parents. Generous guy, I thought. Great family. Lovely wife.

The girls had on headphones in the back seat. Riding along, I thought we'd pass the time with small talk. So I asked Ray a few simple questions about how he had gotten his start in law, where he grew up, where he went to school. Ray's thoughtful, profound, and at times gut-wrenching answers left me gobsmacked. I was speechless. I won't spoil why Ray's story is so inspiring just yet. You'll have to read on and hear it from him. Ray has been gracious with his time, his answers, and his life story. I learned that Ray's is a life well lived. Strong character, deep resolve, a true inspiration. Ray Sanseverino is a true and profound success. Now it's time to find out why. Enjoy.

Chris Dessi: You passed the bar exam in 1973, and you're currently Chair of Loeb & Loeb's Real Estate Department. How did you get there? What was your path to success like? Tell us about that journey.

Raymond A. Sanseverino: During my senior year at Franklin & Marshall College, I decided that I wanted to go to law school. When I got to Fordham Law School, I decided that since I was going to practice law for the rest of my life that I should excel at it, so I worked hard. It helped that I found my passion because I love what I do. My first job after graduation from Law School was at Rogers & Wells (now known as Clifford Chance), which at the time was headed by Bill Rogers, who had served as Attorney General and Secretary of State of the United States under different administrations. After about three years there, I became anxious for advancement and considered leaving. I was comfortable at Rogers & Wells, had high ratings, was well-liked, and I was treated very kindly. There was a certain security in working as an associate at a large firm, but to keep the peace among all of the associates, the firm had to treat those in the same class somewhat equally in terms of compensation and partnership opportunities. After I had decided to leave Rogers & Wells, my first interview was at a tiny firm of 4 partners, one of whom, Sol Corbin, was especially impressive. I was told by Sol that I would not have to wait the then-typical seven years to be considered for partnership and that I would not be held back by big firm rules and procedures and salary constraints, that I would make it—or not make it—purely on my own merits. The firm would not have to limit my advancement for the sake of keeping peace among other associates, for there was none!

As I pondered the move, the decisive question I asked

myself was "in 5 or so years, do I want to be known as Ray Sanseverino, partner of Bill Rogers, or do I want to be known as Ray Sanseverino, great lawyer?"

When I answered the question that I wanted to be known for what I had accomplished, rather than feeding off someone else's glory, I left Rogers & Wells and joined Corbin & Gordon. I was

Ray in his Office

made partner there two years and three months later. I was five years out of Law School. Several clients to which I was assigned to do work at Rogers & Wells followed me to Corbin & Gordon, which was a wonderful surprise and made me realize that despite my lack of social or business contacts, I could develop a law practice based on the quality of my work and superior client service. As I began to handle transactions on my own, a number of my adversaries hired me after the transaction was done to handle other deals for them. The path that I envisioned for myself when I made the move worked extremely well for me. I was judged and treated solely based on my performance without the constraints of the large firm structure, and I was incentivized to work hard and build a practice.

About three years after I became partner, we renamed the firm Corbin Silverman & Sanseverino LLP and I became its managing partner. I held this position for 15 years, until we merged our practice into another firm, where I stayed for four more years. Then, I joined Loeb & Loeb LLP in August 2006 with two of my partners from Corbin

Silverman & Sanseverino.

Chris Dessi: How much of your success was due to luck? Or are you of the mindset that you create your luck?

Raymond A. Sanseverino: I firmly believe that luck is the residue of design; it does not happen unless you put yourself in a position to succeed. Having said that, I was lucky to be born in the greatest country in the world, where opportunities are limitless.

Chris Dessi: Did you have a mentor? How important do you think mentorship is for young executives?

Raymond A. Sanseverino: I did not have a mentor in the formal sense that someone took me under his wing and said I will help you, but I had mentors in the sense of various role models starting with my mother, then one or two partners at Rogers & Wells and Sol Corbin. I watched them and learned from them. Having a mentor is certainly helpful, and I think some need it more than others, but one can learn from observing how others navigate life and business and then emulate them.

Chris Dessi: When did you first think of yourself as a success?

Raymond A. Sanseverino: At the end of my first year of Law School, when I ranked 4th in my class, was invited to join The Fordham Law Review and won several awards for academic excellence.

Chris Dessi: You have three amazing daughters and a wonderful marriage. Many young executive struggle with work life/balance — myself included. What advice do you give them? How did you strike a balance?

Raymond A. Sanseverino: Striking the proper balance is most difficult. You have to determine what is most important at a given time in your life and career and how much money is enough. To me, my family is the most important aspect of my life, and my children have given me more joy anything else. So I decided to make them my priority through their early teen years, at which time they wanted to spend more time with friends and their own activities. I had my first two children when I was very young, 22 and 27, and I did not spend much time networking and entertaining clients through their formative years. I decided that I would build my practice later when they were older. Now that I have a 7-year-old daughter, I cut back on my networking activities a bit to give her the time that she needs from me. I can do a lot of my work at home and I need little sleep, so I try to get home to spend time with her and work later after she is sleeping. I also have a very understanding wife, who often receives the short end of the stick. But whether or not you achieve the balance is really determined by the members of your family.

Two incidents told me that I had succeeded in balancing work and personal life. First, when my younger (now middle) daughter was age 12 or 13 she told that she wrote about me in one of her class assignments. She said, in part, that "my dad always has time for me even though he is in all those books." When I asked her what books, she said you know, Who's Who in America and Who's Who in American Law. She understood that it takes a lot of time, effort and hard work to be recognized as an outstanding lawyer, but that I was always there for her.

The second incident was when my oldest daughter told her husband that when they had children, he would need to travel less to be able to attend their children's events. He said, "I see how hard your dad works, he must have missed a lot of your events." She said, "no, he never missed a play, a concert or a dance recital that I was in."

Ray with his wife Kimber, and daughter Sophie

Chris Dessi: On paper your resume reads like success, after success. Can you tell us about your biggest failure? How did it change you or shift your approach moving forward?

Raymond A. Sanseverino: I do not think that I have suffered any material professional failures. On the personal side, my biggest failure was the dissolution of my second marriage. After my first wife had died, I remarried a little more than two years later as I wanted to restore for my then young daughters and myself the family unit that we had lost. The marriage was too soon after my first wife died and the woman I married was not the right person for me. That failure caused me to be too cautious in my personal relationships and perhaps too analytical.

Chris Dessi: Who has been the greatest positive influence on your life? Tell us about that person.

Raymond A. Sanseverino: My mother is the strongest person I know, mentally and emotionally. She is a fantastic mother whose devotion to my sister and me was and is unwavering and rock solid. My mother never said no to any need that my sister or I had, no matter our age or circumstance. Although I learned many crucial life lessons from my mom, I do not recall her telling me how to conduct myself, but rather she taught me by example, by how she conducted herself, which she did with a great deal of grace and dignity. I learned perseverance from her — never quit until you have achieved your goal. I learned the importance of dealing with adversity, for life is full of adversity. Had my mom succumbed to adversity, I know I would not be where I am today. She had many obstacles to overcome and difficulties to endure in raising two children alone on a low paying secretary's salary, commuting several hours a day from Uniondale, Long Island to Brooklyn so that we could live in a suburban home. Yet, I never heard her complain once about her lot in life nor did she ever utter the word quit. She raised my sister and me without any rancor, but instead, with a huge amount of love and an abundance of selflessness and an indefatigable spirit. I learned from her that there is no excuse for failure. No one is interested in excuses why something was not done. I remember all of the commendations my mother received from her employer for excellence in performance and attitude. I learned commitment, responsibility and sacrifice from her stellar example.

Chris Dessi: What do you think is the one characteristic that all the successful people you know share?

Raymond A. Sanseverino: Determination coupled with a willingness to work hard. I do not know anyone who is successful who does not work hard. Not all, but many successful people (myself included) have to push themselves beyond their comfort zone to achieve their goals.

Chris Dessi: You have 20 minutes to sit alone in a room with the 21-year-old Ray Sanseverino. He's about to embark on a phenomenal career, but he will soon see tremendous adversity in his personal life. What advice do you give him?

Raymond A. Sanseverino: Persevere. You have overcome much in your 21 years to get where you are today. Do not let personal adversity stop you from achieving your professional and personal goals. Equally important, find a vocation you are passionate about and you will never work a day in your life.

Chris Dessi: You're an Italian-American guy. You were raised in a blue collar environment. You have navigated in a white collar conservative professional environment most of your professional life. Have you ever had to overcome discrimination?

Raymond A. Sanseverino: Yes. Although I was at the top of my class, was Articles Editor of The Fordham Law Review, wrote three articles that were published in the Fordham Law Review (when only a few students publish just one), and won seven awards for academic excellence — I could *not* get an interview at several major New York law firms. Although it was not said, I believe it was because of my heritage. I also think that Italian-Americans have had to overcome the perception that most are related in some way to mobsters. Often, when people think of Italian-Americans, they think of Tony Soprano (or real life mobsters). It is an image I feel that I have had to fight for years, one that I detest. When I think of Italian-Americans, instead, I think of Justice Scalia, Justice Alito, Da Vinci, Michelangelo, Dante, and Christopher Columbus, just to name a few greats. I am quite proud of my heritage, but that is not the perception others have of us.

Chris Dessi: I speak with many successful executives that

question the value of college. You're very active with your Alma Mater Franklin and Marshall, and you have a JD from Fordham. What do you say to those detractors of education? I guess what I'm asking is — what did you get from your education, and do you think it's all worth it?

Raymond A. Sanseverino: A college education is so worth the time and expense, especially a rigorous liberal arts education, like the one I received at Franklin & Marshall College. There, I was taught how to think, to see the world in new ways, how to write, how to communicate, how to analyze situations, how to find solutions. I was exposed to great literature, brilliant minds, and I was launched into a life of meaning and achievement. It shaped me into an educated and engaged citizen and prepared me for the rigors of law school. College helped me to mature, and it provided many leadership opportunities, which have served me well. I do not believe in those who say "college is not for everyone." To the contrary, I think it is for everyone, and it is not just about whether it will enable you to obtain a high paying job.

Although F&M certainly launched me into a trajectory of success, college is more about helping to make you a more informed person and a better citizen in a democratic society. Fordham Law School taught me how to think and analyze like a lawyer as well as the substance of the law. I believe in this so much that I put my money where my mouth is. I have endowed a scholarship at Franklin & Marshall for needy students, and I support Fordham Law School. I am eternally grateful to both institutions and extremely proud to have received degrees from them.

Chris Dessi: How do you define success?

Raymond A. Sanseverino: Achieving a high level of

197

satisfaction with your professional and personal life. Being happy every day.

Chris Dessi: For someone who has seen great monetary success — what do you think is the most dangerous thing about that type of success?

Raymond A. Sanseverino: Forgetting how you got there and where you came from. I never forget and often remind myself of the days when spending 25¢ to buy an ice cream cone for my daughter was a significant decision.

Chris Dessi: How important are habits and routine to your success? What is your Rhythm? What time do you go to bed? Do you exercise? Do you meditate? Do you pray?

Raymond A. Sanseverino: While I find comfort in habits and routine, I do not view them as important to my success. But I do think it is important to exercise as it brightens my mental outlook and enables me to work long hours. Typically, on Sunday to Thursday nights, I go to bed between 1:00 am and 1:30 am and typically I wake about 6:30 am to swim laps in my pool (from May to October) or to work out on my Elliptical machine before going to work. I do not meditate, but I do pray.

Chris Dessi: I know you were a star athlete in high school and college. How important have athletics been to your success?

Raymond A. Sanseverino: Very important. First and most important, athletics enabled me to go to college. Also, I learned things on the athletic field that I could not have learned in the classroom, things that become part of you, that define you, things that once you learn it and live it, you know of no other way. I learned tenacity, overcoming obstacles, discipline, and persistence. I learned the importance of doing it right. Sports is a great equalizer. No matter what your socio-economic background is, the playing field levels everyone.

Chris Dessi: I know that your father left you at a young age. I also know that you lost your first wife to a car accident, which left you badly injured. How have those defining moments, and your home life afterward affected your career success? Has it helped you, or hindered you? Tell us about overcoming that adversity.

Raymond A. Sanseverino: I think those moments have actually helped me, not that I would ever choose to go through them. But, knowing that I have succeeded professionally and personally despite great adversity has given me the strength and courage to face any obstacle, knowing that nothing in front of me likely could be as difficult as what I faced previously and overcame. My childhood circumstances made me determined to excel, to work hard, never to have to scrape by. The death of my first wife (whom I had dated in high school) was devastating to my family and me. There were days when I did not want to get out of bed, but I had to survive for my two daughters, so in the end, I refused to give up or to be beaten back, although that would have been the easy course. I remarried a little more than two years later, which turned out to be a bad decision, but I kept my focus on my law practice and my two daughters through lots of difficult and tumultuous times with my ex-wife. All of those experiences have made me stronger. Flourishing, despite lots of adversity, gave me the confidence that I could overcome anything. As a result, I fear no obstacle.

Chris Dessi: I know you as a humble person, but I need you to brag a little here. What has been your greatest success to date? Tell us about it.

Raymond A. Sanseverino: On the personal side — raising two loving and wonderful daughters who are smart, ambitious, driven, and high achievers — helping to raise a third (she is not yet 8 years old) — being able to buy a house for each of my mother and sister — providing financial support for my mother — and being able to endow a scholarship at F&M for students in need. All of this has given me more satisfaction than I can describe. Professionally, building a very large practice without any social contacts or family connections, but purely by the quality of my work and unparalleled client service, and being recognized by clients and my peers for the quality of my work.

RAPID FIRE

Chris Dessi: My daughters know that I hate witches — what's one thing that scares the hell out of you?

Raymond A. Sanseverino: I would not want anyone to know.

Chris Dessi: Best day of your life?

Raymond A. Sanseverino: Each of the days that my three daughters were born.

Chris Dessi: Worst day of your life?

Raymond A. Sanseverino: 5/24/80, when my first wife and I were driving to Manhattan for dinner, and we were hit broadside by another vehicle and she was killed and I was in the hospital for three weeks.

Chris Dessi: You have access to a time machine, but you can never come back to present day. You can go into the future, or into the past. Where do you go in time?

Raymond A. Sanseverino: To 1787, when the United States Constitution was being drafted.

Chris Dessi: Name someone who knows more about you than anyone else in the world.

Raymond A. Sanseverino: My wife, Kimber

Chris Dessi: Most powerful book you've ever read that you recommend to everyone.

Raymond A. Sanseverino: It is a play actually: King Lear, by the greatest writer in the history of the world, William Shakespeare. If I had to pick a book, it would be D-Day by Stephen Ambrose.

Chris Dessi: What's one word that your wife would use to describe you?

Raymond A. Sanseverino: Intense

Chris Dessi: If you could share a meal with any four individuals, living or dead, who would they be?

Raymond A. Sanseverino: Jesus Christ, Ben Franklin, William Shakespeare and Michelangelo.

Success Habits of a
New York Legend:

ROSANNA SCOTTO
Anchor of Good Day New York

Some guys have all the luck. I'll never forget the first time I sat on the Good Day New York couch with Rosanna Scotto. Partially because her co-anchor Greg Kelly scared me, and partially because I think I fell (just a bit) in love with Rosanna. Don't worry — my wife is well aware of my infatuation. I remember Rosanna being welcoming, warm, and at ease in her own skin. It struck me that she wasn't a TV personality. That she is a professional reporter who happens to be on television. I think there are a select few who have that "it" factor. That ease of personality while on air. Oprah comes to mind. It's about four or five years since that first appearance. Greg still sorta scares me, and my infatuation with Rosanna has shifted to full-on *awe*. She's the type of woman you want your daughters to look up to and the type of role model that New Yorker's can be proud of. She's a joy to be around, and a true New York success story. Please welcome — New York legend — Rosanna Scotto.

Chris Dessi: Rosanna, I didn't grow up there, but I was born in Bay Ridge, Brooklyn. You grew up there. I've lived in Belgium and London, and even after I tell people I didn't grow up there — all they want to know about is Brooklyn. Hollywood loves Brooklyn too. What is it about Brooklyn that you think people are so drawn to?

Rosanna Scotto: I think Brooklyn has the great American story...rags to riches. . from Barbra Streisand to Jay-Z. Plus, the people who grew up there have a genuine authenticity with no tolerance for BS.

Chris Dessi: The first time we met was on the "Good Day New York" set. I remember it well. When asked by friends and family what you were like all I could remember was being gobsmacked by your beauty. You're a gorgeous woman, in a male dominated environment (media). How has this shaped

Greg Kelly, Rosanna Scotto, Chris Dessi

your career? I mean this seriously. Do you feel it helped you starting out? Has it hindered you? Do you find yourself cringing when you see News Anchors that look more like models than journalists?

Rosanna Scotto: You are way too kind with the compliments. When I was starting off in the business, I was told to concentrate on the content, not my looks. I wanted to find that exclusive story. I made my name by reporting the big stories. My suggestion is that if you want longevity in this business you better back up that beauty with hard work.

Chris Dessi: I have a great deal of respect for what you and Greg do every day on "Good Day New York." Why do you think that combination works? How much of that dynamic combo was luck?

Rosanna Scotto: Greg and I didn't know one another when we were assigned to "Good Day New York." It took months of getting to know each other on and off the air. We both gave each other room to grow. Our roles have since evolved, as we've worked together for three hours a day, five times a week, and 40-something weeks a year. We have so much fun that we can forget that we are on the air. It may have been luck that brought us together, but it sparked a great chemistry.

Chris Dessi: More than anyone I've seen on TV (other than your co-host Greg Kelly) people who see you on TV get the sense that they know you. You have a way of fully being yourself on air. Many are drawn to you. Does that come naturally to you? Or did you learn that somewhere along the line? What I mean is — when did you first say, "I just need to be myself" and this whole thing will click.

Rosanna Scotto: My bosses always told me to be myself. That is one of the hardest things to do. It took me years to be comfortable with myself and to be willing to show the good, the bad, and the ugly. I was afraid to make mistakes and afraid to really let the Brooklyn accent come through. It wasn't until I let loose did I see a change in the way people respond to me on the street. They like that I'm not perfect. Thank GOD!

Chris Dessi: Have you ever felt that you've burnt out? That you no longer want to be on air? If so, what else would you do, and why? I guess I'm asking — what else are you passionate about?

Rosanna Scotto: I'm so lucky that I have a job that is so different every day. We cover news, politics, and lifestyle. I have a front row seat to history because I get to interview the people everyone talks about. In fact, some of our interviews get people talking! I'm allowed to explore my passions by booking some of those people on our show. Whether we're talking with Donald Trump or interviewing the chef from a neighborhood restaurant, I'm learning something new every day and that is so exciting.

Chris Dessi: You always have a great deal of energy on air. What's your daily regimen like? Do you work out daily to help? Or is that just your gear? We see you on air early every morning. What's your daily rhythm? What time are you in bed, what time do you wake up?

Scotto Family

Rosanna Scotto: I try to have a routine...9:00 — 9:30 p. m. to bed and up at 4:30 a. m. I like to work out at least three times a week. I tend to be very energetic naturally, so that helps fuel this job.

Chris Dessi: You've managed to have one of the most successful careers in media, and you've raised two amazing children. How did you do it when they were younger? Were there times when you felt like you couldn't do it? Was your husband supportive or your success? If so, do you think it's paramount to have a supportive spouse as you make your mark in this world?

Rosanna Scotto: I'm so happy that I am married with two children, but balancing motherhood and work is challenging. My husband and I always worked at it. When my children were younger, and I worked 3 p. m. — 11 p. m. I volunteered at their school and went on every school trip. I would always come home for dinner and help with homework, and then get back to work around 8:15 p. m. My husband took over at that point. It's not easy to have a family and career but at the end of the day, it's so fulfilling.

Chris Dessi: Tell me about the rough patches? What were they like? How did you survive them? What has this journey been like for you?

Rosanna Scotto: I have worked my way up the TV news ladder. I started off as a desk assistant, moved on to researcher, field producer, reporter, then anchor. I lived in Atlanta and worked my way back to New York City and Fox 5.

I have been passed over for many job opportunities. Luckily, I have a family that believed in me, and I was able to stay focused and land the anchoring job. It may look easy, but those of us who do it day-in and day-out know that you have to be dedicated to staying alive in this business.

Chris Dessi: For young female journalists starting out — what advice do you have for them?

Rosanna Scotto: Work on getting contacts and making sure

that your story has information that the competition doesn't.

Chris Dessi: Have you always wanted to be on television?

Rosanna Scotto: I wanted to be an actress when I was younger but realized TV news was more exciting. And stable.

Chris Dessi: What do you consider your biggest success thus far?

Rosanna Scotto: Greg and I took a 5th rated morning show and brought it to #1. We are the little engine that could.

Chris Dessi: What has been your favorite/most embarrassing/worst on-air moment?

Rosanna Scotto: Too many embarrassing moments to talk about, but if you Google Scotto and soy, let me know what you think!

Chris Dessi: Best day of your life?

Rosanna Scotto: Giving birth to my children

Chris Dessi: Worst day of your life?

Rosanna Scotto: covering the 9/11/01 attacks

Chris Dessi: Those who read my blog know that my Father has been a huge influence on my life. Is there someone in your life that had helped to define the woman that you've become?

Rosanna Scotto: My parents have always been a huge source of encouragement.

Chris Dessi: How do you define success?

Rosanna Scotto: Success is feeling comfortable in being

who you are, and waking up happy.

SPEED ROUND

Q. Coffee or Tea?

A. *Coffee.*

Q. Katz's or Carnegie Deli?

A. *Carnegie — they have a sandwich named after me.*

Q. Favorite Restaurant (other than Scotto's obviously)?

A. *Other than Fresco by Scotto, Da Silvano.*

Q. My daughters know that I hate witches. What (if any-thing) used the scare the hell out of you as a kid?

A. *Bozo the clown! I have a picture of me with Bozo and I was crying.*

Q. Do you have a saying that is your life motto?

A. *We are not quitters.*

Q. What keeps you up at night?

A. *A full stomach!.*

Q. When did you first consider yourself a success?

A. *When I was invited into Billy Joel's dressing room.*

Q. Can you speak Italian?

A. *No.*

Q. If you had a time machine what year would you visit, and why?

A. *I love the 40s because of the clothing and music.*

Q. Godfather, or Goodfellas?

A. *Goodfellas.*

Q. Best concert you've ever been to?

A. *Billy Joel and Paul McCartney.*

Exclusive Secrets from a Polymath CEO

DENNIS SIMMONS
CEO at Wasc Holding LLC

I'm a good neighbor. I plant flowers in my yard. I smile and wave hello. I offer to help to move furniture. But, the main thing that makes me a good neighbor, is that I mind my own business. That is until I met my neighbor Dennis Simmons.

I remember the first time I saw Dennis. I was standing in my kitchen sipping a fresh cup of coffee. I had been out late the night before with my wife. It was a Saturday morning. My wife woke up early with the girls, and let me sleep in. When I looked out the window and saw Dennis, I thought

I was still asleep. He was wearing a red car racing jump-suit. I blinked my eyes to confirm what I was seeing. Yep. Red jumpsuit. Now, I don't know the technical term of the outfit, but I could tell it was for racing cars. There I was, hungover, sipping coffee after having slept in late, peering out my kitchen window like the neighborhood gossip. And there was Dennis — across the street, getting out of his Audi sports car in a racing jumpsuit. A real life James Bond, to my real life hung-over schlub. Apparently, he had been a bit more productive with his Saturday morning than had I. Oof. I was overcome with both curiosity and jealousy all at once. Who was this guy? What car was he racing? Why was he *racing*? What does he do for a living? We had been living across the street from Dennis for months, but I had never had a real conversation with the guy. We were only ever friendly. I decided that needed to change. My wife and I have since become dear friends with Dennis and his lovely wife, Laura. I was curious about Dennis then, and I remain so today.

As our friendship has grown, my curiosity has deepened. He is a true renaissance man (don't roll your eyes). This guy is the real deal. He's a powerhouse intellectual, who happens to be a CEO. Who is a passionate wine connois-seur & collector. Who races cars from time to time. That enjoys scuba diving (even though it used to terrify him). Who is in better shape than most people 1/2 his age because he bikes more miles on weekends than I drive. Who's also a musician. The list goes on. And on. And ON. Every time we meet for a double date, I grill him. You did what?? Why?? How?? For how long?? Wait. WHAT? Start that story from the beginning, etc, etc.

A few weeks ago we were at dinner. We were drinking some of his amazing wine. Of course, I was grilling him, when it dawned on me — I need to share Dennis with the world. This dude is fascinating. His life and the way he lives his life have inspired me. The way he shares his success and supports those that he loves is exemplary. He's just one of those guys. I love him. You're gonna love him too. Wait until you read about Dennis's Grandson Reese. Read on, and enjoy.

Chris Dessi: In the process of your amazing career you've been able to travel the world. Was traveling always your goal, or did travel just manifest because of your profession? Tell us about that journey.

Dennis Simmons: I grew up in a military family with four other siblings, and we were always moving from Air Force base to AF base. In fact, I went to 10 different schools my first 12 years. You learn very quickly to make friends as they might not be there tomorrow. Our family lived for several years in Germany. I traveled extensively throughout Europe as a teenager, and it was a real eye opener for me.

After undergraduate school, I served (drafted) in the U. S. Army. I was stationed stateside for several years (missed Vietnam by ten days). After active duty, while serving in the reserve after active duty, I spent part of the summer of 1980 in Germany on the border between West and East Germany (before the Berlin Wall came down) for REFORGER

(Return of Forces to Germany), a cold war exercise sponsored by NATO. I was the "official" tour guide for a number of soldiers who had never been out of the U. S.

Finally when I had a chance to take my family overseas in 1986, I took it and traveled to the Middle East! We spent 5 ½ years there, and that was a springboard to traveling all throughout Europe, Africa, and the Far East. The world is full of beautiful, interesting people and places. I always say my children no longer belong to me but belong to the world! I continue today to travel outside the U. S. with my new wife. Laura and stepson.

Chris Dessi: I speak with many successful executives that question the value of college. What do you say to those detractors of education?

Dennis Simmons: I went to undergraduate school as I thought that was what you were supposed to do when you finished high school. It took me two years to figure out what I was doing there. I nearly flunked out my freshman year. I did, however, make the Dean's list the last two years! Seven years later I went to graduate school for an MBA at night for three years while working a full-time job and that was a different story. It was not just about course work and assignments, but real life experiences from my professors and most importantly my fellow classmates — all executives, engineers, and professionals.

Chris Dessi: How do you define success?

Dennis Simmons: Success to me is contributing to something (whether a service or product) that benefits a person or a group of people. And if you are lucky, sometimes it is recognized and acknowledged by your peers.

Chris Dessi: Can you explain the impact, if any, that social networking/digital media has made on your business/career or you personally?

Dennis Simmons: Funny you should ask this while I was in the Middle East, I utilized the first email provider Compu-Serve. With a satellite uplink, I was able to communicate back to the US for work and then ultimately my family.

Personally, I have learned over the last few years that social media is a great way to stay current with my kids and friends. I continue to work on the whole social media area with my profession; healthcare and all its rules and regulations about privacy. We are making progress. I have learned a lot from attending the Westchester Digital Summit twice (not just a plug but the truth)!

Chris Dessi: How much of your success was due to luck? Or are you of the mindset that you create your luck?

Dennis Simmons: I believe that you have to create your success. You have to position yourself to try new things, different experiences, both professionally and personally. Sometimes just being in the right place at the right time helps, but you have to be prepared to jump out of your comfort zone and take a risk!

Chris Dessi: Did you have a mentor? How important do you think mentorship is for all executives?

Dennis Simmons: Yes, two professors in undergraduate school, one professor in graduate school (the Dean of the business school), and one person professionally who convinced me to go on to graduate school and obtain an MBA while I was working full time. I received an award (unofficial) from those two professors after graduation from Texas A & M (I am an Aggie!); "Most likely to succeed, if he can ever decide what he wants to do!"

Having mentors was truly motivating for me; it inspired me and drove me not to let them down, but ultimately not to let myself down! I consider myself to be very lucky to have had/have them.

Chris Dessi: You participate in some of the most compelling and intriguing hobbies outside of the office (music; playing drums and guitar, racing cars, bike racing, scuba diving). Is this activity born from a conscious decision to be active? Or is this just the way you're wired?

Dennis Simmons: I learned at an early age that music was very important to me. I started playing drums in the third grade. I picked up guitar in high school. I played in several bands growing up in Europe and stateside. I own several drum kits and many guitars! Being active was always a mindset. Whether it is Scuba diving in the Red Sea, Persian Gulf, or Caribbean, or riding in a 220 mile charity biking event, tandem skydiving, playing paintball, zip lining in Costa Rica, rappelling out of a helicopter, teaching Spinning or racing cars with Skip Barber — I have always enjoyed being active and trying crazy things. It is my makeup (sounds a little cosmetic)!

Chris Dessi: When did you first think of yourself as a success?

Dennis Simmons: Probably in 1983-84, when a small group of people and I in Austin, Texas began working on the STARFLIGHT (Shock Trauma Air Rescue) project, a city/county and local hospital joint venture for a medical helicopter rescue program. The program successfully got off the ground in 1984 after many, many late night meetings, spanning over a year, and working with numerous elected officials (City and County) for funding. The program continues today as one of the premier air rescue programs in the United States.

Chris Dessi: You have amazing kids and a wonderful marriage. Many young executives struggle with work life/balance — myself included. What advice do you give them? How did you strike a balance?

Dennis Simmons: I recently remarried in 2012 to a wonder lady, who like I, struggles with the balance between work and personal life. My only advice is to find that balance and practice it daily. Decide upon a cut off time for work and head home. They are always going to be sacrifices, but take the time you have with your family and maximize to its fullest extent when you are not at work or even thinking about work! Always be present!

Chris Dessi: On paper your resume reads like success, after success. Can you tell us about your biggest failure?

Dennis Simmons: In 1996, I came to New York with a start-up PPM (physician practice management) company that ultimately went public. I thought it was a great opportunity to build something from scratch. But I learned in short order that the founders were not interested in developing a long-term company, but just wanted to make a quick buck. After less than two years, I left, and several years later the company ultimately collapsed. I had to rebuild a large number of professional relationships and start over. That took me more than a year.

Chris Dessi: How did it change you or shift your approach moving forward?

Dennis Simmons: I have kept to smaller projects with more extensive due diligence on the principals and partners.

Chris Dessi: Who has been the greatest positive influence on your life?

Dennis Simmons: There have been many, but at the top of the list is my grandson Reece!

Chris Dessi: Tell us about that person.

Dennis Simmons: Reece was born with Cerebral Palsy 10 years ago, and he has been a true inspiration to me and every life he has touched. I will never forget the day when my daughter called after Reece was born and said something was wrong with him. He was soon diagnosed with Cerebral Palsy. But Reece was about to make his impact on the world. No matter what the situation, no matter what he does, there are no obstacles to him.

His every action no matter what he chooses to do he is so damn positive, you look at yourself in a mirror on a bad day and say, what do I have to complain about?

Quick story, last Christmas I bought him, his uncle and mother a helicopter tour of Houston to see the Christmas lights. Reece loves experiences rather than toys! When they showed up at the airport in North Houston, a lady asked what was he afflicted with? His uncle said "CP." Reece said, "Yeah but it doesn't bother me!" That response blew her away! He is one amazing young man! My Hero!

Chris Dessi: What do you think is the one characteristic that all the successful people you know share?

Dennis Simmons: Not worrying about what other people think of you. Be yourself and don't be afraid to speak your mind and try different things!

Chris Dessi: You have 20 minutes to sit alone in a room with the 21-year-old Dennis Simmons. He's about to embark on a career that will take him around the world. What advice do you give him?

Dennis Simmons: Eyes and ears open, work hard, learn to work in a team setting and surround yourself with smart people. Place a high value on personal and professional relationships. Don't take them for granted!

Chris Dessi: For someone who has seen great monetary success — what do you think is dangerous about that type of success?

Dennis Simmons: Take nothing for granted, it could all change tomorrow.

Chris Dessi: How important are habits and routine to your success?

Dennis Simmons: I have always tried to accomplish something each and every day. Whether it was something large or small, just something to hang your hat on each day! I also try and do something personally to help someone each and every day.

Chris Dessi: What is your Rhythm? What time do you go to bed? Do you exercise? Do you meditate?

Dennis Simmons: I am an early morning person (5:30 AM), so I try and get to bed by 10:00 PM. Though I must say the advent of iPads has affected that goal. I have been a cycling (Spinning) instructor for over 16 years. I have lifetime certification. I do exercise regularly and especially enjoy riding my road bike.

Chris Dessi: How has your childhood (the way you were raised, your birth order) affected your career success? Did it at all?

Dennis Simmons: My father instilled in me a very hard work ethic! Both in his military and professional career he worked incredibly hard. Work was the center of his world, and it clearly rubbed off on me. I look forward to going to work each and every day!

Chris Dessi: I know you as a very humble person, but here is your chance to brag a bit — what has been your greatest career success to date?

Dennis Simmons: I came to New Jersey in 1999 to take over the opening of an ambulatory surgery center (ASC) with just nine investor/partners. I was only to be here for two years. Since that time we have built a company with over 58 investor / partners and have outlasted the "average" ASC. Stats reveal that a mature multi-specialty ASC will only last ten years. Well, 16 years later and more than 110,000 surgical cases performed, we are a very strong company. And 2015 is turning out to be an amazing year for the company. Our same stores grow is in excess of 13 % while most centers are experiencing negative grow.

RAPID FIRE

Chris Dessi: My daughters know that I hate witches — what's one thing that scares the hell out of you?

Dennis Simmons: I fear suffocating. It was difficult for me to learn to Scuba dive, as I was totally afraid of suffocation and not being able to breathe under water. Remember your mother always told you to hold your breath when you put you head underwater. I had to unlearn that skill. I ultimately became a PADI Certified Divemaster 25 years ago.

Chris Dessi: Best day of your life?

Dennis Simmons: Every day of my new marriage and watching my children/grandchildren grow up!

Chris Dessi: Worst day of your life?

Dennis Simmons: In 1991, while stationed in Saudi Arabia, the first Gulf War was about to start, and we were told by our embassy and the Civil Aviation authorities that the civilian airport would remain open, should the war start. I wanted to be sure that if we needed to get our families out of harm's way, the airport would be the first option. Well, I took that info for granted and when the coalition forces started the bombing campaign the airport was closed. Thus, my family had to endure several nights of warning sirens, Scud missile attacks and Patriot missile launches. I was so mad at myself that I allowed this to happen. I remember walking out of our villa one morning and collecting pieces of missile parts with my youngest daughter after a horrible night of missile attacks.

I remember being confronted by British troops walking through our compound after one horrible night while we were collecting pieces of a Patriot missile. The soldier told us we couldn't have any of the pieces. I explained to him that it was made in the U. S. A. , and, therefore, I could have it!

After a couple of nightmare nights, I called in a big favor from a gentleman who worked for a major aircraft man-ufacturing company, and he was able to get my family out of harm's way on a non-scheduled flight / unmarked airplane out of Saudi Arabia. They had to leave first thing in the morning basically in their pajamas to get on the flight. I didn't know for 24 hours that they made it back to the United States safely. And thanks to the kind heart of an American Express agent, I finally talked to them at an Air Force base in Kansas and also get them a new AMEX card so they could catch a commercial flight back to Texas and buy some clothes.

Chris Dessi: You have access to a time machine, but you can never come back to present day. You can go into the future, or into the past. Where do you go in time?

Dennis Simmons: Future, after I am long gone from this world, I want to know that my kids and my grandkids are doing alright!

Chris Dessi: Name someone who knows more about you than anyone else in the world.

Dennis Simmons: Laura, my best friend, companion, and wife.

Chris Dessi: Most powerful book you've ever read that you recommend to everyone.

Dennis Simmons: Yeager: An Autobiography.

Chris Dessi: Worst city you ever visited?

Dennis Simmons: Juarez, Mexico.

Global Success Forged by Ingenuity & Work Ethic

TOM SHINE
Serial Entrepreneur, Co-Founder Logo Athletic, Executive Leadership Reebok, XIX Entertainment, Angel Investor

The first time I met my brother-in-law Tom Shine was memorable (for me anyway). We'd both been in San Franciso on business. We knew we would be on the same flight from San Francisco to Florida, but we'd never met in person. Tom (then an executive at Reebok) had invited the family to join him at the annual NFL coaches meeting in Florida. Because the family would all be there, I saw the trip as an ideal time to pop "the question" and make Tom's sister in law, Laura, my wife.

Tom was sitting in first class. I recognized him from photos. But his head was down reading as I boarded. I kept walking and didn't introduce myself. I didn't want our first meeting to be awkward or in the aisle of packed airplane. Instead, I waited until we landed. I needed to make a good first impression.

Stepping off the plane, I extended my hand smiling "Hi Tom, I'm Chris." Tom replied, "What the hell? Were you sitting in the last seat of the plane? I've been standing here for 20 minutes." I chuckled and replied sheepishly, "As a matter of fact, I was."

Great first impression Chris.

It's a silly story, but I always thought that the metaphor of our first meeting was fitting for my relationship with Tom. In my mind, he's up front in first class. Not even aware that he's in first class because it's become so normal for him, — while I'm in the last seat. . . waaaayin the back. When you're in the last seat, all you want to do is sit in first class. Or at least figure out how the guys in first class got there. So when I get his ear, I grill him:

- How many years did it take you be successful at Logo Athletic?
- What was it like to sell your business to Reebok?
- Did you take investors at first or did you boot strap?

I already knew Tom was a huge success before I first met him, even though he's not loud or ostentatious about his success. There is a deep, *deep* center of confidence and knowing about him. That special "something" only the most influential in our culture have. He commands your respect and attention. The type of guy that chats up a garage mechanic with the same aplomb and enthusiasm as a billionaire NFL owner. A rare breed for sure.

Tom's a serial entrepreneur whose inner circle includes Hall of Fame football players and entertainment icons. He's also one of the most generous and down to earth people I've ever met. He'd kill for his family & friends. Because of Tom, I've been on the field during Indianapolis Colts games, and I've been to a Super Bowl. He's been known to fly family members to Mexico and Hawaii without flinching.

Like others I've interviewed here, he's been around the world three times over. He does so with a contagious energy and enthusiasm. He's functioning on an almost super-human level. Able to shun jet lag, and attend his daughter

Morgan's soccer game an hour after landing from Europe.

The last time I was at his home in Indiana, he offered me some amazing advice about business. We were having a compelling conversation about entrepreneurial life when he did something that stuck with me.

While heading home from an event with the whole family, he took an abrupt detour. Driving past a run-down building in downtown Indianapolis, he pointed. He said, "that was the first office of Logo Athletic" (the company Tom later sold to Reebok). He assured me that if he succeeded as an entrepreneur I could too. Wow.

Tom is a self-made man. A person I admire and respect. While some of his peers are retiring, Tom Shine is just getting started.

Chris Dessi: How do you define success?

Tom Shine: Defining success is extremely difficult because what is successful for one individual may well not be successful for another individual. Success has many different tentacles to it — financial, emotional, reputation, credibility, etc. An outside force might look at a person who has had financial success and believe that individual is successful while many of the characteristics of how they would define it for themselves has not been met. Success is relative to where you set your goals and what you want to accomplish in life.

Chris Dessi: I speak with many successful executives that question the value of college. What do you say to those detractors of education?

Tom Shine: I do *not* believe that college is for everybody. I think barring a profession that requires a college degree (i.

e. medical, law, etc.), one can very easily make a case that the time and the money spent in college could be better spent in an entrepreneurial or career building direction.

Chris Dessi: You have one of the most vast and impressive networks of business people I know. Was that intentional, or has that network just grown organically? How important has this network been to your success?

Tom Shine: One of my initial goals from the very beginning was to build as strong a Rolodex as possible. I have worked and networked those relationships every day that I have been in business, believing that one relationship leads to another. I don't think that there is anything more important than building up those connections and at the same time, working and maturing those connections so that they can be utilized when called upon.

Chris Dessi: Can you explain the impact, if any, that social networking/digital media has made on your business/career or you personally?

Tom Shine: I can honestly say that I am from a generation, which is one step removed from the social media explosion, which in many cases, is greatly overstated. It has had little to no effect on my business, with the exception of allowing me more flexibility and accelerating communications.

Chris Dessi: How much of your success was due to luck? Or are you of the mindset that you create your luck?

Tom Shine: I am of the mindset that you create your luck. Certainly there are instances where luck has prevailed, but I think those are the exception, not the rule. In general, hard work, preparation, commitment, focus, and perseverance are the underlying factors.

Chris Dessi: Did you have a mentor? How important do you think mentorship is for all executives?

Tom Shine: I had several mentors, and I can't emphasize enough how important mentors are. Mentors allow you to avoid costly financial and time-consuming errors, have an important voice in important decisions. I have found that in the last several years, the upcoming generations do not embrace mentors and hence, they are going to go through life taking the longer and more difficult route.

Chris Dessi: When did you first think of yourself as a success?

Tom Shine: Unfortunately, I first thought of myself as a success when I was able to purchase items that I had long desired. I found out shortly after that the items were meaningless, and the goal had been set way too low.

Chris Dessi: You have three amazing daughters and a wonderful marriage. Many young executive struggle with work life/balance — myself included. What advice do you give them? How did you strike a balance?

Tom Shine: I think one of the things that entrepreneurs do is convince themselves that they are doing this for their family, when in truth, they are doing it for themselves first and their family second. That type of thinking causes some difficult decisions and some difficult priorities to be made; often at the expense or priority of the family. One of the difficulties that happen in a first marriage is that the individual has a tendency to grow in business and success, while at the same time; his wife and family are growing and achieving success in their own theatre. It is extremely difficult to try and keep those connected, and you can find that the two can grow apart very quickly. There is a very good chance that if there is a second marriage, the individual has most likely reached a level of success and a life pattern, which is not emerging but set. It is easier to strike a balance with work and family on the second relationship because the first is almost always building and changing and less in control of your personal time.

Chris Dessi: On paper your resume reads like success, after success. Can you tell us about your biggest failure? How did it change you or shift your approach moving forward?

Tom Shine: I would say my biggest failure in life was my first marriage. I was always under the impression that you got married, and life just followed a normal path. What I didn't realize was that marriage is like everything else, something you have to work at. The failure of a marriage has a significant effect on many important people in your life. I think it taught me a lot of lessons in life and taught me how to address my future relationships in a more involved and considerate manner.

Chris Dessi: Who has been the greatest positive influence on your life? Tell us about that person.

Tom Shine: I don't have one person — I have several people. One is my grandfather, Morris Kaye, who taught me the value of hard work. My father, who taught me the value of relationships. Earl Harris, of Paul Harris retail stores, because he challenged me to the point you felt like you were in graduate school every day. Mel Simon, who taught me the importance of being a visionary and risk taker. Herb Simon, who taught me the combination of all the above.

Chris Dessi: What do you think is the one characteristic that all the successful people you know share?

Tom Shine: A significant work ethic.

Chris Dessi: You have 20 minutes to sit alone in a room with the 21-year-old Tom Shine. He's about to embark on a career that will take him around the world. What advice do you give him?

Tom Shine: Identify whether you want to have your signature on the front of the check or the back of the check. After you have made that decision and assuming it's the name on the front of the check, you will need to determine that you are willing to pay the price that's to come with the pursuit of entrepreneurship.

Chris Dessi: For someone who has seen great monetary success — what do you think is dangerous about that type of success?

Tom Shine: The only risk I see is losing the perspective of who you are as a person.

Chris Dessi: How important are habits and routine to your success? What is your Rhythm? What time do you go to bed? Do you exercise? Do you meditate?

Tom Shine: I am not sure if a routine is the right word, but there are certain habits that are extremely important. Keeping yourself in mental and physical balance is important, and exercise is paramount. Everybody is different — I prefer to operate on 5-6 hours of sleep a night knowing that I can physically outwork anybody.

Chris Dessi: How has your childhood (the way you were raised, your birth order) affected your career success? Did it at all?

Tom Shine: I think I was raised in an entrepreneurial family from my grandfather on down. The work order and work ethic were very clear. I don't think the birth order had any effect on success.

Chris Dessi: You're Jewish, and you were raised in Indiana — have you ever had to overcome discrimination?

Tom Shine: Absolutely. There are several examples, but I don't think it has anything to do with Indiana, it has to do with being Jewish. Ignorance doesn't know state boundaries.

Chris Dessi: I know you as a very humble person, but here is your chance to brag a bit — what has been your greatest career success to date?

Tom Shine: My greatest career success was starting a company and the # of people I was able to employ for significant lengths of time. In other words, at the 30th anniversary of our company, I had 22 people that had been employed since the inception of the company and a very large number of employees at 25 years of employment. One of the best ways to judge the success of your company is how you treat your employees.

RAPID FIRE

Chris Dessi: My daughters know that I hate witches — what's one thing that scares the hell out of you?

Tom Shine: Snakes!

Chris Dessi: Best day of your life?

Tom Shine: Everyday

Chris Dessi: Worst day of your life?

Tom Shine: The day it ends

Chris Dessi: You have access to a time machine, but you can never come back to present day. You can go into the future, or into the past. Where do you go in time?

Tom Shine: In the future — the unknown intrigues me.

Chris Dessi: Name someone who knows more about you than anyone else in the world.

Tom Shine: My middle child, Lindsi Shine.

Chris Dessi: Most powerful book you've ever read that you recommend to everyone.

Tom Shine: Steve Jobs book (http://amzn.to/1WD7dpt).

Chris Dessi: Worst city you ever visited?

Tom Shine: New Delhi, India

The Ultimate Guide to Success Survival & Redemption from Former President COO of Monster Worldwide

JIM TREACY
Public Speaker, Writer, Consultant and Former President and COO of Monster Worldwide

James Treacy, former chief operating officer of recruitment services giant Monster Worldwide Inc. (AP Photo/ Louis Lanzano)

first met Jim Treacy last year through a trusted client and friend <u>Vikki Ziegler</u>. Within the first 20 minutes of knowing Jim, we became fast friends. Jim was forthright, intelligent, and warm. He had a humility that didn't fit the man's accomplishments. He had reverence for our team at Silverback, and assured us that he was there as a student of social media. He then articulated his vision for his business partner. I hung on every word for the next two hours. I cherish moments like that. When I meet someone that's whip-smart, and with that much business experience, I shut up and listen. I too had lived through the DOT com boom of the late 90's and early 2000's, but I hadn't experienced half of what Jim had. As Jim and I spoke, we realized that we shared mutual acquaintances. We bonded on our shared similar assessments of their personalities. I knew I liked Jim immediately.

It's been my goal for my "Success" features to include individuals who have seen more than monetary success. Those who could add a different assessment of the success they've seen in their lifetime. After seeing astronomical monetary success, Jim faced jail time and almost lost it all. While it's easy to sit back and ponder how we would handle ourselves in a similar situation, I can't help but think that it would break many of us. After meeting Jim, I can tell you that it has only made him stronger. He has a clear vision for his future. A strong moral compass, and an infinite thirst to keep growing, learning, and connecting. That's the type of success I'm looking for. That's the kind of success I hope finds you as you read this. Jim's Q/A is a riveting look into the excesses and successes of the DOT com world. Enjoy this one, it's a gem.

Chris Dessi: You were the President and COO of one of the most wildly successful DOT com's of all time. How did you get there? What was your path to internet stardom? Tell us about that journey.

Jim Treacy: It was 1994. I was 36 years old. To date, I had a highly-successful career — corporate officer since age 28, decent money, people under me — a veteran player in a headline-making <u>hostile</u> <u>takeover</u> and likewise for a billion dollar <u>debt restructure</u>. One day a headhunter called me up about a CFO position at a cash-strapped, advertising agency backwater called TMP Worldwide (today called Monster Worldwide). The position was beneath my accomplishment, but I was feeling under-appreciated and bored where I was, so I took the meeting. They offered me the job immediately. I politely turned them down.

Months later, the entrepreneur, more riverboat gambler, who owned the bulk of TMP, called me up and invited me to dinner. During the meal, he pitched me the CEO position with equity ownership of the company's fledgling, money-losing, Recruitment Advertising division. The proposal was to team-up and do a classic debt-financed roll-up. He'd buy them; I'd fold them in. I accepted the challenge and, in just two years time, we turned that small unit into the world's largest Recruitment Advertising agency.

Jim and his middle daughter

During that frenetic build, I was introduced to the Internet. I had no idea what it was. Serendipity occurred during a late — 1994, California, budget meeting. An acquisition we were folding-in showed me an in-development web-site, Career Taxi. It took an hour of some very patient explanation and demonstration for me to understand the huge opportunity being presented.

If we could convince all the clients in my division to place their job ads on an Internet site we owned, rather than place them in printed newspaper help-wanted sections, we could go from being an ad agency to a publisher. Meaning instead of making fifteen cents on every client ad dollar (the other 85 cents went to the newspaper), we could keep it all. As they say, a no-brainer. I tripled their development budget, on the spot. Then, once back in New York, I spent the next several months, with help from others, getting the big boss (Mister Roll-Up) to understand the concept. When he finally got it, he bought up nascent career-sites The Monster Board and Online Career Center — both for a song — before 1995 was out.

The rest is history. Right time, right place and a huge existing client base to introduce our wholly-owned web-sites too — vision, execution, a bit of luck, etc. Over the next few years we went public, moved those clients online and melded our various career sites into one big powerhouse, Monster.com. It became the number one, global, Internet career portal by a wide margin. Our eclectic management team, for a time, got to be Wall Street darlings. Most impressively, of the hundreds, maybe even thousands, of commercial websites launched during the late-90's on into the great Dot Com crash of March 2000, Monster was one of the few significant, stand-alone, Internet businesses, alive and well out the other side of the meltdown (2002). Along with Amazon, Yahoo, eBay, Match, Priceline...keep going if you can. I don't think you'll get to much more than ten examples. I'd note we were added to the S&P500 Index during the crash, May 2001.

Chris Dessi: I speak with many successful executives that question the value of college. What do you say to those detractors of education? You did your undergraduate work at Siena, and you have an MBA from St. John's. Can you point to a time when you felt you HAD to have an MBA? How much has your MBA contributed to your success?

Jim Treacy: A college education is neither an obligation or a right. 1 Not everyone is cut out for college. If you like and have the skills to work with your hands, there is a lot to be said for controlling your own destiny as a plumber, electrician, mechanic, etc. — always in demand, no college debt burden. Also, I'd argue a Navy or Air Force technician, for those high-powered warships or planes, is a great base to build a lucrative, post-military career off of. Plus you got paid and saw the world while becoming an in-demand tech expert.

Now, if you decide you are college material be warned that it is an expensive privilege, not a right. There are many ways to finance it, none easy. So if you want or need the degree be a grown-up and have a realistic plan on how to make it happen for yourself.

With those disclaimers out of the way, you asked the "value" question. Hopefully your readers can forgive a sports analogy. LeBron James came out of high school ready to storm the NBA, but he's an extreme aberration. There are very few high school basketball players prepared, mentally or physically, to go straight into the NBA, Ditto for football/NFL and baseball/MLB. Most all these guys must continue developing and proving themselves at the college or minor league level before even having a shot to make it in the big money, win now, professional leagues. No one coddles you in the pros — perform or you're out & quickly forgotten. I don't see preparing for Corporate America much differently. It's also an extremely competitive world.

So if you're asking in the Peter Thiel "college is often a waste of time" sense, I wholeheartedly disagree! Thiel is way brighter than me, his book "Zero to One" has a lot of good stuff in it and I respect his libertarian bent, but I firmly believe college is an invaluable experience for many.

Yes, Mark Zuckerberg, Steve Jobs, Bill Gates, etc. never completed college but, like LeBron, they're "freaks of nature". Guess what? 99. 9% of us aren't that. College provides a nurturing environment — both inside and outside of the classroom — to grow and develop as a complete person, academically and socially; a chance to learn and make "harmless" mistakes, in a fully supportive environment, read community. America's global leadership, as well as the vast number of international students that flock to our college and university admission doors attests to that value.

Regarding my MBA: I had a great deal of fun in my undergraduate time at Siena — particularly outside the classroom. As my senior year began the job market stunk, my grades weren't much better, and I hated my major as career. That's when I decided a Masters Degree was in order. The value of my MBA was it got me to a major I enjoyed and could happily build a career on, gave me some post-college time to get my "serious" hat back on and opened doors for positions that required such. Glad I did it.

Chris Dessi: You lived through the wild west of the internet. Of all the characters you've come across — who pops into your mind as a person that you knew was going to be a success? Why? What talent/attribute did they have?

Jim Treacy: Two come-to-mind, at different junctures, for generally the same reasons, from roughly the same position in the room when I noticed them.

The First: I was Treasure Americas for the WPP Group, finishing up the last complicated piece of a long-running billion dollar debt restructure — a $250 million asset securitization — including instituting a mutually acceptable, daily-reporting structure for said lenders. We were working with a team from Prudential Securities. In large group meetings, I tend to give short shrift to all the pontificating. Instead, I study the work product presented and who actually did that work. During this process, a young kid on Prudential's team stood out. He was smart as a whip, appropriately but not overly deferential to rank, fast and accurate on the work product. I thought, "He'll do well." Years later, as an Internet analyst at CIBC Oppenheimer, he made a headline-making bullish call on Amazon's stock price, in the face of much media skepticism. He was proved right in just three weeks. Today he's the Co-Founder/CEO/Editor-In-Chief of *Business Insider*, Henry Blodget.

The Second: I was the EVP/Finance & Strategy at Monster Worldwide. Morgan Stanley led our 1996 IPO and 1997 Follow-On Offering. Thus, I was in seemingly endless meetings with groups of Morgan Stanley employees. Once, after such a meeting, I witnessed a young fellow get a terse "to-do" listing from Morgan's brilliant and driven, Internet analyst, at that time, Mary Meeker. I thought, "This poor kid won't sleep tonight." I ambled over and made a crack about the treatment, adding if anything on his list was TMP-related never hesitate to call me for assistance. His immediate response was as mature and as thought out as any I'd ever heard. He smiled, thanked me and said something along the lines of, "Oh, Mary's all-right. She's under a lot of pressure to be perfect all the time. This is my two years in the army and having this on my resume will open doors." In 1998, he was hired away, by Amazon, to head their

Investor Relations efforts. Today, he's Amazon's SVP Kindle Content. You may, or may not, have heard of him, but I guarantee everyone in the publishing world knows who he is. And, after 17 years at Amazon, my guess, he's also a very wealthy guy, Russ Grandinetti.

Chris Dessi: How do you define success?

Jim Treacy: If you enjoy the people you are surrounded by and are 100% at ease looking into a mirror. 1

Chris Dessi: For many of my readers public speaking is a great fear. But you do it so well, and often (television, etc). How do you do to prepare for public speaking? Have you been trained, or does it just come naturally?

Jim Treacy: I've never had, or was much interested in, formal public speaking training. So, I guess it's natural. When I choose to speak it's on topics that I'm passionate about, as well as experienced and knowledgeable in. I try to know a bit about the audience, in advance. This allows pre-thought on how best to engage them. No matter the situation, I speak my mind, sugarcoat nothing and let the chips fall where they may. My tone and message are the same whether I'm talking one-on-one, to an auditorium full of people or in front of a camera. Total comfort in my beliefs, nary a worry if they please or pain.

Chris Dessi: I have two young daughters. What advice can you give them that if I share this with them in 10 years you think will translate to their success?

Jim and his Wife

Jim Treacy: Failure is not a sin; failing due to lack of preparation or effort is. Whatever you want in life, whatever challenge you take on, give it everything you've got. If you know you couldn't have prepared any harder, given an ounce more energy on the drive to the goal; you'll be fine. In fact, that maximum effort, more often than not, will generate success. On the odd occasion where you truly prepared, gave top effort and still failed I guarantee a valuable life lesson will reveal itself. It'll sting but, if you embrace it, you'll become smarter and stronger for the next challenge.

Chris Dessi: You're pretty candid about your time in jail. How long did it take for you to be so comfortable with sharing that time of your life with people?

Jim Treacy: Instantly, I did zero wrong. The whole thing was a career-enhancing farce for a few despicable prosecutors and a scrapbooking judge. I've talked and written at length about it. Sadly, America's justice system has turned into a massive, wealth-creating industry. An ugly one where prosecutors act with impunity, eye on million-dollar law partnerships or high political office; pampered, lifetime-appointed judges rule to political agendas, and prisons are valued as blue collar job creators that also line many a politician's pockets. *The Economist* ran a very insightful, October 2014, cover story, on the whole systemic mess

Chris Dessi: Did you have a mentor when you first started out? Do you think mentorship is important for all executives?

Jim Treacy: I can name people who assisted me all along the way. The list is long. If, as a person, you don't merit colleague assistance your career will be in flames.

Regarding a classic mentor/mentee relationship, that occurred in my second employment stop, The Ogilvy Group. I was fortunate that the Chairman/CEO, Bill Phillips, saw something in me. For whatever reason, he made sure I had a variety of opportunities to stretch myself. I appreciatively latched on to each one. In my experience, a natural, not forced, mentor match is extremely helpful to an executive's development.

Chris Dessi: When did you first think of yourself as a success?

Jim Treacy: One of my grandfathers was a longshoreman on the docks of the Westside of New York City — Hells Kitchen. The day I showed him my Ogilvy business card that said "Vice President" he smiled ear-to-ear, grabbed it and quietly stuck it in his wallet.

Chris Dessi: Who has been your greatest positive influence on your life?

Jim Treacy: There're a few ways to take that question. My parents for a stable, supportive environment to grow up in. My wife and kids who keep me grounded. Or from study: Jesus Christ for "do unto others," Abe Lincoln for having the courage to work with a Team of Rivals and George Patton for the merits of audacity in battle.

Jim with 2 of his 3 daughters in Paris

Chris Dessi: You have an active social media ecosystem, and you're a blog contributor for the Huffington Post (Business Insider contributor, as well). What do you say to executives who think that they don't have time to be involved in building their personal brand online?

Jim Treacy: If you don't define yourself somebody else will do it for you. Also, if you've had some success it's nice to share it; be part of the conversation.

Chris Dessi: What do you think is the one characteristic that all of the successful people you know share?

Jim Treacy: Energy. They make things happen. No sitting around with expectations of a handout or perceived entitlement.

Chris Dessi: What advice do you have for Mark Zuckerberg if any?

Jim Treacy: I had the pleasure of sitting next to Mark at a 2006 luncheon. I wrote an article about it. He's a nice and very successful fellow, playing at an IQ level way above mine, thus needing no advice from me. But forced to offer some, it would be, "Keep going, you're absolutely killing it! From a very happy, long-term shareholder."

Chris Dessi: For someone who has seen great monetary success — what do you think is the most dangerous thing about that type of success?

Jim Treacy: Sometimes those with a great deal of money equate that with what they perceive to be their own brilliance or superiority. Pure nonsense. I know a lot of classless dummies with coin and many classy people with not much. Circumstance, luck, what you value, etc. all play a role.

Chris Dessi: How important are habits and routine to your success? What is your Rhythm? What time do you go to bed? Do you exercise? Do you meditate?

Jim Treacy: Very. Type A, all the way. Typically, by 11 PM. Most everyday, a five to seven mile run. While I get a lot of reflection in during my daily run, I do not meditate in the traditional sense. However, when at our LBI home, I am known to sit on the beach, cooler at hand, and silently watch the waves break for hours on end.

Chris Dessi: How has your home life affected your career success? Were your parents strict? Do you have brothers and sisters? If so, how have they affected you and your drive to succeed?

Jim Treacy: The people in my life have always been hugely supportive of me. I very much appreciate, and some-times wonder, how they tolerate me. When "I'm on/in the game" I can be insanely competitive, opinionated, cocksure, driven, laser-focused…a little nuts, frankly. Fortunately, the things that turn me "on" I keep to a short list.

I wouldn't refer to my parents, whom thankfully are still around, as "strict." I'd use the word, "disciplined". They are both salt-of-the-earth, blue-collar, dyed-in-the-wool, patriotic Americans, as well as devout Roman Catholics. They set an excellent example and provided great opportunity.

I have two sisters, both younger. One has a Ph. D. in Mathematics and is a highly successful educator. The other is a Manager, Cloud Enablement & Engagement at IBM. Proud of them both. The "disciplined" construction worker and homemaker did alright rearing their flock of three.

Chris Dessi: You're a very active Board Member, advisor, and investor in many companies. What advice do you give to young entrepreneurs who are looking to get funded?

Jim Treacy: Distraction is doom! Entrepreneurs are ideas people. Often they just keep having them, never staying focused long enough to see one through to full fruition. I try to explain, "You've got this great concept, defined its success, the money crowd is interested, now you have to focus and execute on that alone." Money flows to rapid results; drifting execution gets impoverished.

Chris Dessi: I know you as a humble person, but I need you to brag a little here. What has been your greatest career success to date? Tell us about it.

Jim Treacy: I firmly believe that nothing great is accomplished alone. Having said that, I was an integral part of Monster's success. Wall Street seems to have validated that. The day I quit the company, August 6, 2002, its stock price plunged a jaw-dropping 30%. One Internet analyst wrote, in a widely-distributed report, that I was "the glue that held Monster together." Modesty should forbid, but he may have been right. LinkedIn launched in 2003 and, in relatively short order, dislodged Monster from its leadership position in the online career sector, bringing on its inglorious banishment from the *S&P500 Index*.

RAPID FIRE

Chris Dessi: Will you ever write your memoirs about the wild days of the DOTcom boom?

Jim Treacy: Will a bold publisher — or producer — with vision appear? Already outlined, 100 hours of taping complete, rich characters, names, historic events; crazy ride. Contract to Best Seller in six months. Ten year Netflix series &/or full-length movie a breeze.

Chris Dessi: My daughters know that I hate witches — what's one thing that scares the hell out of you?

Jim Treacy: "Smile for the camera." I get self-conscience posing for pictures. A pariah in this "selfie-world."

Chris Dessi: Best day of your life

Jim Treacy: June 15, 2011, roughly 7:00AM: Processed out of the crater called Morgantown Federal Correctional Institute — liberty restored, in college ball-playing shape, having hurdled Uncle Sam's senseless mind-game. Blue sky, beautiful wife beaming across the parking lot, my Uncle Pete holding a cup of real coffee aloft, my kids and home just a half-day drive away, George Harrison's "Here Comes the Sun" running through my brain...

Chris Dessi: Worst day of your life?

Jim Treacy: No contest, "9/11." I was downtown with roughly 120 Monster employees. A terrible scene. Stays with you. As many did, I lost some friends and acquaintances that day. NYFD Chaplain, Fr. Father Mychal Judge, OFM, being one — from my Siena College days; wonderful soul! *(Authors Note: The photo below is of Jim on September 11th — When the planes hit on 9/11 Jim was at the Embassy Suites — a short block from the North Tower1 — giving a talk to 120 Monster employees, from around the globe, in a leadership seminar. They headed up the West side along the Hudson — below is a photo — taken by a Goldman Sachs analyst who was with Jim for the talk. The photo is right after Jim was having a roll call taken to ensure everyone from Monster is accounted for — see the woman with her hand up, as in here).*

Chris Dessi: You have access to a time machine, but you can never come back to present day. Where do you go in time?

Jim Treacy: As a big fan of *just* insurrection, two events pop-up. From my non-violent side, the Last Supper. I would have had a few questions. From my combative side, the Continental Congress. I would have been all in.

Chris Dessi: What advice would you give to the 16-year-old Jim?

Jim Treacy: Be 100% true to your true self, 100% of the time and all will come well!

Jim was President and Chief Operating Officer of Monster Worldwide. He joined Monster's predecessor, TMP Worldwide (a 27-year-old, cash-strapped, private entity), during 1994, as Chief Executive Officer of its smallest division. In 1995, Jim played an integral part in identifying and rolling-up the nascent websites that would morph into Monster.com. During this time, he formulated and executed the cross-selling strategy known as "Feed the Monster," which ultimately estab-

lished Monster.com as the leading global Internet career portal and validated the online recruitment industry as a credible, vital and growing segment of the global economy. Learn more about Jim here and follow him on Twitter here (https://twitter.com/jimtreacy).

Adrian Dessi

The Quaz has never been about fame.

I've never sought out Julia Roberts or David Wright or Jimmy Carter; never hoped that (golly gee!) Halle Berry or Brad Pitt or Ray Rice will grace me with 15 minutes for my stinkin' blog.

No.

I began the Quaz 100 interviews ago because I'm genuinely fascinated by people, and I prefer asking questions to answering them. I want to know how it feels to be a valet parking attendant and not get a tip. I want to know what it's like, being a firefighter and climbing into a burning building. I'm intrigued by elation and rejection, heartbreak and overwhelming love. I always tell my students (100 times per class) that being a journalist is a *gift*, in that you have license to ask people almost anything you want. "That," I shout, "is a beautiful thing!"

The first 100 Quazes have been a mishmash of people from mishmash walks of life. Guitarists like John Oates, Tommy Show, and Bruce Kulick; four of Kevin Arnold's love interests from the Wonder Years; a KKK leader, Miss Black Iowa, a childhood friend fighting through MS, a woman blogging courageously about cancer, an opera singer, a street musician, a Tea Party activist, 12 former Major Leaguers, an erotic escort, a professional skeptic, a bashful illiterate from Little House on the Prairie, the CEO of Panera, the only woman to score a point in Division I football, a dog trainer. Some have been great, some have been meh, but I like to think they all pay homage to the power of curiosity.

This week, for the historic-only-to-me 100th Quaz, I wanted someone special. I've fielded countless suggestions, but never one that truly moved me. Then, a few weeks ago, I thought about my boyhood on the mean streets of Mahopac, N. Y. Specifically, I thought of a man who seemed to somehow have this life thing figured out, even from the heartbreaking nest of a wheelchair.

I grew up with Mark and Chris Dessi, and consider both to be good friends. Four years ago, their father, Adrian Dessi, was first hit with the idea that he might—*might*—have ALS. The initial symptoms of Lou Gehrig's Disease can be vague and misleading, so it's difficult to diagnose. Ultimately, Adrian's symptoms could not be dismissed. He was experiencing, among other things, muscle twitches and fatigue.

Indeed, it was ALS.

Now 67, Adrian Dessi is extraordinary. I visited him at his home in Camel N. Y. on a cool Thursday last month, not quite sure what I'd find. Would he be depressed? Solemn? Would he cry? Bemoan the inevitable lost years?

Two words: Hell. No.

Adrian and Patricia at their wedding on Aug. 16, 1969

Meet my new hero—a man who overcame a rough childhood filled with ritual beatings and dismissive parenting. A man who turned darkness into blinding light. He is the father of two, the grandfather of five, a successful businessman, a loving husband, an ALS sufferer and, oh, yes, stronger than steel.

Adrian Dessi, I am honored to have you as the 100th Quaz.

Jeff Pearlman: How did you become aware that you had ALS?

Adrian Dessi: I had a heart murmur. In the fall of '09, I went for my physical, and the internist says, 'You have to go see the cardiologist. Your heart murmur has gotten worse. ' And at the same time I complained to him about getting muscle twitches. He said, 'Go see the neurologist" So I went two paths—neurologist, cardiologist. I wasn't thinking ALS. Cardiologist comes back and says, 'The heart murmur is bad. If you don't take care of it and get valve repair or replacement, you're going to have serious damage to your heart. ' OK, I go to the neurologist down here, he sends me down to Cornell Weill, and I come back after that. He says, 'Well, it's possible-to-probably ALS. ' This is the fall of 2009. So I said to him, 'How many people have you diagnosed with ALS?' He said, 'You'll be the second. ' I said, 'OK, time for a second opinion. ' Plus, when you have an ALS diagnosis you don't go for heart surgery. So we went down to Columbia Presbyterian, to the Lou Gehrig neurological unit, and we met their team, went through their battery of tests, which were a little more extensive than the ones I got previously. And they came back and said, 'Gee, we don't think you have ALS. We think you might have benign fasciculations—the muscle twitches. And two weeks later I had my heart valve repaired.

This was now January 10. I had the surgery in Westchester, near White Plains. So I come out, luckily they didn't have to do a valve replacement. They were able to repair the valve. I come out of the surgery, and I say to my wife, 'I can't cough. I can't sneeze. ' She said, 'Tell the doctor. ' OK. Every morning a team of doctors comes in, checks me after the heart surgery. 'How you doing?' I say, I can't cough. I don't have the diaphragm. That's what happened. The surgery, your body goes through trauma during open-heart surgery. The trauma exasperated the ALS in my diaphragm. But I didn't know it. I did very well with the heart surgery recovery. Within a matter of three, four weeks I was going three days a week to a cardio unit for exercise. Where they monitor you. They're tracking you as you exercise. They increase the times, the duration, the kinds of exercises. All I kept getting were accolades. 'You're doing great! You're doing great!' But I'm saying to myself, 'If I'm doing so great, how come I have to hold onto the handrail to lift myself up the five steps to get into the place?'

Jeff Pearlman: Were you thinking about ALS again?

Adrian Dessi: I wasn't thinking about anything. All I was thinking about was my body … something's going on. This is not right. I'm saying to people, 'I have benign fasciculations. ' But you've been in the gym — you know what it is to feel your body increase. You increase your breathing capacity, your stamina, your muscle strength. You feel it. Here I am, going to cardio physical therapy three times a week, 45 minutes each time, and after three months why can't I walk up four steps? It was like, something's going on.

Adrian with his sons, Mark (left) and Chris.

On top of all that, I have a bad disc. I had lower back pain. So my internist suggested, 'You need physical therapy. ' So now I'm up to five days a week. Three days with the cardio, two days a week with the physical therapy. I come home; I lay down on the couch, I collapse. I'm out. My wife's coming home from work, she's like, 'What the fuck is going on? You're sleeping in the dark at 4 o'clock in the afternoon. ' I said, 'I don't know what it is. I'm just exhausted. ' It goes on a little bit longer. I'm complaining about my back. Doctor says, 'Why don't you go get an MRI?' Alright, so I get the MRI. Now I'm feeling weaker, and I decide I think we need to go back to the people at Columbia to see what's going on. This is now January 2011. We go back; they check me out, and they say, 'Yup, it's ALS. ' OK. And at the same time, I've got pain here, I've got pain here. And the message I'm getting from the neurologist is that ALS is a painless disease. I said, 'For a painless disease, I'm going through the fucking roof here. This is a bitch. I got pains in my thoracic area, 360 degrees around my body. And I've got pain in my lower back. So they sent me to their pain management group at Columbia. I go there; they look at the MRI, and they know I've just gotten the diagnosis of ALS. And he said, 'Well, if you didn't have ALS I'd be talking to you about disc replacement. Your disc is gone. It's gone. ' So we started a regiment of lower spine steroid injections, and some injects for my thoracic area. So ever since then it's been—I have ALS, and that's it.

Jeff Pearlman: What does it feel like when you hear your diagnosis, and it's ALS? I don't mean, 'Oh, this is horrible. ' Like, how did you process it and did you accept it? Not accept it?

Adrian Dessi: When the first doctor told me, and he said it's possible to probable, I think in my gut I knew it was *probable* more than *possible*. And I accepted it. You know, it's life. You know, how do you accept getting a D on your math exam? It is what it is. You have to deal with it. It was tough telling my wife. I went to the hospital myself;

she was still working at the time. It was tough telling my sons, my daughter-in-laws; it was tough telling my brother, Joe. You know, I told my brother. We were playing golf over in Mahopac. He had come up for the weekend. We were playing, and I said, 'Something's going on, I thought you would like to know. I have ALS' He was like, 'What?'

I don't know how people react to things like that. I didn't break down. I didn't cry.

Jeff Pearlman: No five stages of grief ...

Adrian Dessi: No, no. It was another punch to the belly like any other punch to the belly you go through life with.

Jeff Pearlman: *That's pretty amazing. I mean ...*

Adrian Dessi: You get punched enough, and you stand up and keep going. You just go along with it.

Jeff Pearlman: So obviously it's a famous disease named after a famous baseball player, but how would you describe what it is like to have Lou Gehrig's Disease?

Adrian Dessi: (Long pause) It's a very frustrating disease. Because it doesn't affect your brain, it doesn't affect your heart, it doesn't affect your bowels, it doesn't affect your urinary tract. But it affects everything else. So, like, you have your finger in your mouth (Jeff's note: *He's referring to me, sitting across from him on a couch*). I can't do that anymore. I have an itch above my eye. I can't scratch it. It's extremely frustrating because every aspect of your life that you're so used to doing—you can't do. I'm at the point now where I'm losing the ability to feed myself. I have to have somebody else to feed me. So it's just very frustrating.

Jeff Pearlman: So do you still have feeling in your legs?

Adrian Dessi: You have feeling over your entire body. You can come over and tickle my toes, and I can feel it. I just can't move it.

Jeff Pearlman: Does it feel like you can move it? Like, can you feel your foot right now and feel the impulse to move it?

Adrian Dessi: Um … put your foot on the floor. Now tap your foot. Tap it more. Tap, tap, tap. I can't do that. It's like it weighs 5,000 pounds, trying to do that. I can lift my heel, but I can't lift my toes. My toes—I'm straining right now with every ounce in my body. And I can't do it. There's no pain involved. The foot doesn't hurt. I just can't move it. And if I try to move it, I strain and strain. But it doesn't move.

Jeff Pearlman: And what's your breathing like? (Jeff's note: Adrian has a breathing tube beneath his nose)

Adrian Dessi: When I came out of the surgery, I lost about 40 percent of my diaphragm. I'm now down somewhere around 30 percent. That's why I use this. It's not oxygen— it's just air. It's what they call a BiPAP machine. What the BiPAP does is it inhales and exhales for you. And it's set to the amount you need to expand your diaphragm. This is what's keeping me alive. I could probably survive without it, but I'd have to use other muscles to try and suck in the air. So there'd be a lot of strained breathing, and what that does is it easy exhausts you. Because it's not a natural muscle. You get heavy breathing when you're running, you stop or slow down and take a breath. Sitting at rest, you're OK. Well here, sitting at rest, I'm using all these surrounding muscles, and that exhausts you. And one of the watch words for this illness is 'energy conservation.' Don't exhaust yourself. Because it exacerbates the situation.

I don't know how much you want to know about the disease. Wait, Jeff, do me a favor and remove this pillow from behind my neck (Jeff's note: *I do*). The disease affects upper motor neurons and lower motor neurons. Basically, that means it's in your brain and it's in your spinal cord. It affects the transmissions from your brain to the muscles, and then back from the muscles back to the brain. The transmission back being disconnected is worse than the transmission going there. And what that means is, when you exercise, the muscles send instructions to the brain, 'Hey, I just got exerted.' And the brain comes back and says, 'OK,' and it does certain things. Without that connection the muscle just lays there, and that's what's happening. Now it doesn't affect every muscle in your body. But what it does affect is the mouth, and a lot of people start with symptoms of slurring words, of dribbling. And they'll gradually lose the ability to speak, the ability to chew, the ability to swallow.

Jeff Pearlman: Will that eventually happen to you?

Adrian Dessi: Probably. Thankfully, knock on wood, I haven't presented those symptoms yet. It's interesting—last month I was out on Long Island, and I met a friend of my aunt's who was diagnosed about a year ago with ALS. She can't swallow; she can't chew. But she stands, she walks, she writes. The disease doesn't attack everybody the same way. Everybody is different. The next big area is the diaphragm. That's my big problem area. The next area is gross motor, and the fine motor, your hands. As you can see, I have trouble with my hands. I can't make a fist or hold a pen. I can barely press the buttons on the remote.

Jeff Pearlman: So does this disease come with definitive moments—Shit, I can't make a fist any longer! Shit, I can't press the buttons on the remote! Shit!

Adrian Dessi: Slowly. This hand looked like this hand two months ago. It's slow, in that it wasn't from yesterday to today. But it's fast, in that six months ago I was able to walk with a walker. Not a lot, but I could walk 25 ... 30 steps. I could stand up. You know, I could feel myself. I could stab something with a fork. I can't do that now. It didn't happen yesterday, but it happens pretty quickly.

Jeff Pearlman: This might sound like a dumb question, but do you wake up in the morning and think, 'Crap!' Or can you wake up in the morning and think, 'This is going to be a good day"? Can you have enjoyment? Is that impossible at this point?

Adrian Dessi: The screwy thing about the disease is it doesn't affect your brain. So I'm the same guy who was playing golf three times a week in 2009. But I just can't do it. There is no ... I'm not in a lot of pain. I'm in pain because I  have disc issues. But other than that, if I'm laying in bed, I'm looking forward to the day. Then you get up, and you deal with the realities. You can't do this; you can't do that.

Jeff Pearlman: So what do you do? What are your days, generally?

Adrian Dessi: My days? Well, because I can't dress myself and bathe myself and feed myself, it takes me the better part of the day just to get up and get washed and cleaned and fed. That's done by 12 ... 1 o'clock. I get up at 9.

Jeff Pearlman: Do you sleep the same as you once did?

Adrian Dessi: I probably sleep a little better. Because I'm tired. There are some nights I sleep like a log. I usually get down around 10, so I sleep from 10 pm until 9 am.

My day ... I watch a lot of TV. I'm a movie fanatic, so I watch a lot of movies. Last night I watched *Prometheus*. I like the concept of the movie because it's based on books I read a long time ago about aliens coming to earth. It was interesting. I probably see six, seven, eight movies in a week. I've seen *Argo, Lincoln, Sliver Linings Playbook, Django*...

I also have two other things that keep my busy. I read. If I decide today I want to get into a book, I'll start today, and I won't stop, and I'll read two-to-three books a week. I have to use a tablet. I can't turn pages. Ask your buddies, Mark and Chris, when we used to vacation down in Florida, I'd take two big thick books, and I'd read them in four days—1,400-page books. I'd hear, 'You didn't read that book!' They'd argue with me. I like to flip through a nice, thick book—start at 8 in the morning, come in at 5 for dinner. But now I can't turn the pages, so I use my iPad. I also have model Lionel trains downstairs. I have a 10-foot x 10-foot table I've been working on for years. It used to be my father in law's set, from the 1950s and 60s. I did a lot with the trains until I started getting severe ALS symptoms. So I pretty much stopped in 2010. But I've been relying on Dwight (Jeff's note: *Dwight is his lovely home health aide*), and my friends who come over, to be my arms and legs. I direct them. My grandkids are beside themselves with it. I just bought a lot of new equipment, and I'm trying to solicit any neighbors who might have free time to help me build. Another problem is access—the only way to get downstairs is I have to go outside and in the back, which means when there's snow on the ground ...

After Chris completed a marathon in his father's honor.

Jeff Pearlman: Lou Gehrig gives his famous speech, *and he says, 'Today, I consider myself the luckiest man on the face of the earth.' Do you get it? Is it possible to feel that way while having a disease like this?*

Adrian Dessi: I'm gonna die. Sooner than planned. 'You plan it, God laughs'—that's an old saying. I went to a support group at Putnam Hospital, and there were people with neurological diseases, and they had a guest speaker who was a pharmacist. And there're about, maybe, a dozen people, and some guests—caregivers. And the majority of the people had Parkinson's. And they're bitching and morning that they shake all the time. 'Why do I have to shake all the time?' and 'Isn't there something I can take to stop the shaking?' I'm sitting there saying to myself, 'I'll take shaking all the time ... I'll give you my right arm and take all the shaking. Because you guys don't know what the fuck you're doing.'

And I've said this to lots of people, and please forgive the language: I'm one of the luckiest fucking guys in the world. I'm a street kid from Brooklyn. You know what that means? It means your expectation is that you're  going to end up like the guy on the corner, flipping half-dollars in the sharkskin suit. Or you're gonna end up, if you're lucky, working in the railroad repair facility right around the corner. I grew up—nobody in my family graduated college. In fact, my mother never graduated high school. Eighth grade—that was it. My father, he was a big shot. He got his high school diploma. So I'm a street kid from Brooklyn. I was blessed. I was 30-years old, I was the vice president of a bank. A half-dozen heartbeats away from the presidency. Making a very, very reasonable salary. And I'm sitting there thinking, 'Where do I go from here?' I had no … it was like, nobody in my family is the vice president of a bank. I mean, my relatives and friends would talk to a vice president of a bank like he was a god. So it was like, 'What the hell is going on here?' So I've been blessed all my life. I've got beautiful sons, my daughter-in-laws are gorgeous, bright young girls. My wife is the love of my life. I mean, I made more money, did more traveling, vacationed in places that I never thought possible. Jeff, we went like half a dozen times and rent a villa in the Riviera. And go for a month with the kids. We had the best freakin' vacations. The place we rented was a friend of a friend's; it was on an acre of land with a big in-ground pool overlooking the Mediterranean, 20 minutes from Cannes, 40 minutes from Nice, 50 minutes from Monaco. We were right there, in Provence. It was unbelievable. You thought you were in heaven. I've been around the world three times. I've done shit, as a kid growing up I would have said, 'You're crazy. Impossible. Will never happen. ' My brother is a former school-teacher. He taught in Long Island for 34 years. He's also a football coach. He coaches seventh and eighth graders. We're talking, he says, 'What was the most amount of money you made in a year?' I told him, I thought he was gonna faint. He couldn't believe it. It was beyond his comprehension. Am I a multi-millionaire? No. But we did very well.

I have nothing to complain about. There's nothing to bitch about. Am I disappointed with this disease? Yeah. What am I disappointed about? See my five grand kids? (Jeff's note: *He motions toward a nearby photograph*). I'm not gonna see them grow up. That's what's disappointing. I have one grandson, Luke. I'm gonna give Luke my golf clubs. I have a brand new set of golf clubs that I think I used a half dozen times. But I'd love to be there when he's graduating high school and say, 'Here kid, these are for you. ' I don't know if I'm gonna be there. I don't think so. He turns 3 in July.

Jeff Pearlman: Do you fear death? Does the idea of death itself make you nervous or uncomfortable?

Adrian Dessi: I don't think about it. It's there, but it's ... I never was the kind of guy that was in my head with my problems. I was never, 'Oh, shit, you lost your job. What will you do? What will you do? How you gonna get a job?' Yeah, I got shot down a lot of times. That's life. My brother tells stories of how he would share my experiences with his friends because he couldn't believe it. He says, 'You lose your job at A, you get your job at B, for twice the money. How the fuck do you do that?' You do it. 'You lose your job with B and you get 50 percent more salary with C. How the hell do you do it?' You do it. Those were opportunities. I didn't set the price scale. They set the price scale. I just had the skill set. He used to crack up. I'd always say, 'Joe, you just go do it. If you get it in your head, you start beating yourself up. That's not the way to go.' I had that as a kid. My parents beat the hell out of me—physically and emotionally. And I learned you can't go there.

Jeff Pearlman: So you're from Brooklyn …

Adrian Dessi: Yes. I'm from Gravesend. I was born in 1945. I went to St. John's Prep. My father was Adrian—I'm a junior. And my mother was Marie. I have an older brother, Joe, and Carol is my younger sister. My father worked in the manufacturing business. He was a clothing cutter. They'd take the apparel, make a suit, you'd lay it out on these long tables; they would lay down on top of that a sample, and he'd come along with a high-speed drill and cut out stacks of materials in the shapes needed to make an arm, a leg, etc.

Jeff Pearlman: Was he a tough guy?

Adrian Dessi: A tough guy? Not really. My father worked in the clothing business, but that's what they used to call a seasonal business. What that meant is he was out of work a lot, so he'd pick up a lot of odd jobs to supplement. And it was a family business, sort of. My grandfather was in the same business, my grandmother was in the same business, my father's uncle was in the same business. But he worked six days a week. Saturdays he would get home, like, 5 o'clock. That was half a day. Because Monday through Friday he would work two jobs. He'd get home, like, 9 o'clock at night after leaving at 7 o'clock in the morning. So I didn't see him much. Saturdays he would come home, he would maybe go shopping with us, then go to sleep. And he slept all day Sundays. It was his day off. So I never really had much of a relationship with him.

Jeff Pearlman: So not a good dad, not a bad dad. Just a dad …

Adrian Dessi: He was … my mother was the disciplinarian. I don't know what kind of upbringing my mother had. But my mother used to beat the shit out of us.

Jeff Pearlman: With a belt? Stick?

Adrian Dessi: More sophisticated. My mother was a thrower, so she threw anything around at you. I got stuck with a fork in my arm from across the table. She threw a steel pot of food at my brother, and luckily he ducked quick enough it went through the regular window and the storm window, down three flights — because we lived on the third floor. She would use broom sticks on us, but then she'd complain to my father that the stick broke. So my father would tell her to get a thicker stick. And one of my father's odd jobs was he finagled himself to become a barber instructor. He never worked as a barber, but he got himself employed where he could get a cushy job teaching people to become barbers. That was his night job. So he worked at the factory cutting material all day, and then in the evenings he would work from 5 until 9, helping people to learn a skill. So what he did is he brought my mother a barber strap. Which is actually like three straps of leather. And my mother used to wear it on her apron. So she'd have it readily available. She would take us into the bathroom. She wore it on her apron, and she also had a hook on the door behind the bathroom and she'd hang it there. She would bring us into the bathroom.

It was interesting, as adults, talking to my brother and my sister about our treatment. They both agreed I got the worst of it because I wasn't the daughter and I wasn't the first son and I was a little bit of an antagonist. I pushed the envelope. Anyhow, that's the bad side. The good side is it made me tough. I have a pretty high tolerance for bullshit.

Throwing out the first pitch at Yankee Stadium in 2011, on the same day Derek Jeter had his 3,000th hit.

Jeff Pearlman: I wrote a book about Walter Payton. His parents would have him go out back and get a stick, then beat him with it. Yet, he loved his parents. Can a mother be that way and also be a good mother? Or no?

Adrian Dessi: (long pause) I don't know what a good mother is. I had a mother. I know what she was. She wasn't a doting, loving person. My father developed a nickname for me when I was a teenager. The nickname was, 'The bum. ' That's how he introduced me. When I was in high school I went to preparatory school, so you had to wear a suit every day; gotta wear a shirt and tie. So I needed clothes, and he was in the clothing business. He'd say to me, 'Tomorrow, come meet me in the office. We'll measure you up for a suit. ' So I'd go, I'm at his work, and I'm meeting all the people he works with. And how was I introduced? 'This is my son—the bum.'

Jeff Pearlman: At that age, did it sting? Or only in hindsight?

Adrian Dessi: At that age it was sort of like, 'What is this a joke? Is this not a joke?' It was water off my back. But you asked about my mother. Move forward. I'm 30-some-thing-years old. Married. Two children. A responsible job at a bank. A 3,000-foot colonial home. Brand new car in the driveway. And my mother says to me, 'Well, maybe you're not such a bum. ' And I said to her, 'You S. O. B. —you meant it all those years. And Dad meant it. ' It wasn't a joke.

My father and my father-in-law were at a family event, and the grandkids were all these, in college. And my father said, 'Boy, we did good. ' And I said to myself, 'What the fuck did you do?' Get the hell out of my house. But I didn't say that.

There was a situation [later on] where I sat down with him with my sister, and we read him the riot act. He said, 'I'm flesh, too! I'm flesh, too!' He was stupid. My mother was also stupid.

Jeff Pearlman: Did you ever forgive your parents? Or now, that they're not here, are you able to sort of, I don't know …

Adrian Dessi: You know, it's so tough. I want to forgive them. Because you need to forgive to move on. At the same time, uh, I did well. I did well. From where I came from, from my family. I remember going to a dance with my aunt and my uncle, my aunt says to my uncle at the time, 'No one makes $100,000 a year. ' I was in my 30s. I was going, 'Holy shit, she doesn't realize I make that kind of money. ' I've done extremely well. Part of that is because I got my ass kicked; because I got my lip broken when my mother threw a metal dish at me three months before I got married. It made me tough, and because I'm tough I'm able to do things.

So on the one hand, yes, I should forgive them …

Jeff Pearlman: But you don't want to give credit for unintended consequences …

Adrian Dessi: Exactly! On the other hand, you say, 'It would have been nice to have had been told that I was a responsible person, that I was a good person. ' I tell my granddaughters—one's gonna be seven, I have two 5-year olds, and I have two littles who are 2 ½ a piece. But I tell the older girls because they can understand. I tell them, 'Tell me what you see when you look in the mirror?' And they say, 'I'm kind, I'm pretty, and I'm smart. ' And my answer is, 'That's right. And don't you forget it every time you look in the mirror. ' I remember as a kid, 8 … 9-years old, looking in the mirror and thinking, 'Who am I? What am I? Except a punching bag.'

Jeff Pearlman: So coming where you come from, how did you escape?

Adrian Dessi: I remember, vividly, I was about 11, and I ran away. I had no money. But I took off. I just ran away. If I had had some money, I would have gotten on the bus and gone somewhere. But I ran away and during that time we lived, literally, by a train yard. It was a depot for the subway system. It's one of the largest ones, down by Coney Island. And I walked that entire facility. I was gone for the better part of eight, 10 hours. And during that period of time I said to myself, 'I'm out of here. I'm intellectually, emotionally, out of here. I don't care what they do to me; I don't care how much they beat me. I'm out of here. ' And I realized the only way to get out was I had to develop skills, and I had to educate myself. But to do that was very tough for me. I had no foundation of support to say, 'You're smart, keep going. ' What I had was beatings. So it was like, 'Why should I get a 90 or 100? I'm going to get my ass handed to me anyway. ' So there wasn't much motivation. I had to become self-motivated for the education. It was not easy because I was an emotional basket case. I went to a Catholic prep school, which you had to pay for. My brother went to Brooklyn Tech, so that was free. For me, I went to Brooklyn Prep, and I thought a little, 'Gee, wow, my parents have supported me. ' But it didn't dawn on me until years later that they didn't do that for me. They did it for themselves.

Jeff Pearlman: Why? Status?

Adrian Dessi: Yeah. They always said, 'You have to go to college. You have to go to college. ' I was an emotional basket case. I got out of high school, I graduated on June 9, 1963. On June 10, I started work. I worked at Steeple-chase. It was an amusement park on Coney Island. The Brooklyn Cyclones' stadium is where Steeplechase was. I started working, and I worked Friday nights from 6-to-1, Saturdays from 12-to-12 and Sundays from 12-to-10. And on Mondays I worked at my brother's old job, in the mail room of a not-for-profit called 40 Wall Street. He got a better job for the summer, so I took over for him for the summer. So I worked Monday through Friday, 9-to-5 on Wall Street. So I proceeded to work 20-straight weeks, seven days a week, working something in the neighborhood of 90-some hours. Why? To save money for college. Because when I got into college, what I got was a handshake from my father. 'Congratulations, I'll sign whatever you need me to sign. ' That was it. So I had to do it on my own. I needed money. Well, think about yourself when you graduated high school. That summer, you celebrated, rejoiced, rejuvenated, then went on to school. I didn't have that opportunity.

So what did I do? I got to school—St. John's University—and I did terribly. I got kicked out in my first year for academics. So my father was there, reinforcing 'My son the bum. ' So I had to get a job, and I got one working in a bank as a teller. Lincoln Savings Bank—the branch on Flatbush and North Street. And I lived at home. And I did that for two, three years. Bought a brand new 1965 Volkswagen Beetle for $1,865. My car payment was $50 per month. I was working as a teller, so I was only making $65 a week. It was tight, but I could do it and I could get to work. And I enrolled in Pace as a non-matriculated student, and I started taking business courses at night. Until I got my grades up sufficiently, and then I quit work, I went to school fulltime and I started working part-time because I still had to pay my tuition. I graduated in 1969. My brother went to college before me, so I was the second in my family to graduate.

Jeff Pearlman: How meaningful was that to you?

Adrian Dessi: It was extremely meaningful to me, because it was the sense of accomplishment. It motivated me to go off for my graduate degree. I have an MBA from St. John's. I went back to St. John's to prove to myself I could get it through there.

Jeff Pearlman: Do you think your parents were impressed when …

Adrian Dessi: I didn't give a shit. I wasn't doing it for them. I was doing it for me.

Jeff Pearlman: Lemme ask this—I always think there are two ways people who are raised by bad parents can go themselves. They can either follow that path or say, 'Fuck that, I'm going to be absolutely nothing like that. ' It seems like you took the second path. Did bad parenting motivate you?

Adrian Dessi: Yes. My brother and I both agreed we were not going to parent the way we were parented. We both agreed we were not going to have a home life the way we had a home life.

Jeff Pearlman: So was it easy to be a different kind of parent? Did it come more naturally to you than you thought?

Adrian Dessi: It was a hard job. A very conscious job. I have to give credit to my wife. My wife is a sweetheart; came from an 180-degree different type of environment. A very loving person, very giving person. It took a lot of her help to help me to see things.

My brother has three kids—his oldest son, Joseph, has his own ad agency. His daughter, Stephanie, has her own occupational therapy business in Manhattan. She specializes in breast cancer victims. His son Matthew is a geologist, but he works for an environmental company, and he's the head marketing guy. And you know my sons. Not too shabby. And they are—all five of them—are aggressive, they're tough business people, and they're loving parents. They all have beautiful kids, great partners. That makes me and my brother and my sister feel so good.

Jeff Pearlman: Like you made it?

Adrian Dessi: Yeah. We … we changed the cycle.

Jeff Pearlman: *What* did Chris running the marathon in your honor late last year mean to you?

Adrian Dessi: It's beyond words. Beyond feelings. I don't know where to begin. It just chokes me up. I mean, for the majority of my life nobody did shit for me. From when I was born, nobody did shit for me. All I got was a 2×4 upside the head and a kick in the ass. To see my son do something for me—I can't put words to it. I'm not used to it. Don't know how to react. You know—never had it.

This disease has a plus side.

Jeff Pearlman: How do you mean?

Adrian Dessi: It's made us all closer. One of the biggest problems I've had in my life is accepting love. I didn't know how to do that. Because what I got as a child certainly wasn't. I got discipline. I was 'My son the bum' to my father and my mother's words were, 'Children are to be seen and not heard. ' And she lived by that. 'Sit there and shut up. You have no point of view. You have no decisions. You have nothing to say. ' So it was difficult. And I had to deal with lots of crazy emotions. I was a pipe smoker for more than 40 years. I loved to go out and smoke. But it was also a crutch. The family would be in the house having a good time; I'd go outside and look in. I couldn't go back in. I didn't feel I was worthy to be inside because I didn't know how to deal with those kinds of emotions. It's taken me a long time. This disease kicked me in the ass in that regard. So it's helped me in that regard. I'm much more open and accepting and understanding.

Intellectually, I don't understand it. But emotionally I'm learning how to take it.

QUAZ EXPRESS WITH ADRIAN DESSI:

Q. Five reasons for someone to make Mahopac, N.Y. his/her next vacation destination:

A. The people, the beautiful lake, the people. I don't know what else.

Q. Do you feel like you abandoned Mahopac by moving to Carmel, N.Y., it's arch-rival town?

A. Uh, no. We don't feel we have because we haven't. We go to Mahopac for everything. I'm a Mahopac guy. When I was 12, my father's cousins used to summer right near Lake McGregor. One summer my father decided to bring us up, and I fell in love with Mahopac. Years later when we were married and looking for a place to live, Mahopac came up, and I said, 'That's the place!'

Q. Best advice you ever received?

A. Be true to yourself.

Q. How often in your life have people made the Rocky 'Addddrrrriiiian!' reference to you?

A. Uh, not as much today as they did years ago. When I was in college I got a lot of them. 'Yo, Adrian!'

Q. How did you propose to your wife, Patricia?

A. We were sitting on the beach on the south bay on Long Island during a sunset.

Q. How did you meet your wife?

A. In college, at a dance at a hotel in Manhattan. I was a super senior at Pace; she was a freshman.

Q. What is the greatest moment of your life?

A. There are two — when my sons were born.

Q. Best movie you've ever seen?

A. Jesus, that's a toughie. I like the movie, what the hell is it, the black-and-white movie … It's a Wonderful Life.

Q. Do you feel like people approach you in a different way now that you have ALS?

A. Yes, they do. And it's very uncomfortable. I would like people to approach me like I'm standing up 6-feet tall, 210 pounds, kick your ass, shake my hand with a nice tight grip. I don't want to be perceived as that sickly old guy sitting in a chair. You know how you get like that, I think? When you start letting this situation take over your life. That's when that happens?

Q. Do you never have 'Why is this happening to me?' moments?:

A. Fleeting. Short. Brief. Kick their ass, get them out of my head. It's really good, because if I let it take hold — and I know this because I'm smart enough to know this — that will be the end. That will be the end of my relationship with my family; it'll be the end of me. And you know what? I'm not dying today, and I'm not dying tomorrow. So fuck you. I don't have time for this shit.